Scribblers

Stalking the Authors of Appalachia

Scribblers
Stalking the Authors of Appalachia

STEPHEN KIRK

JOHN F. BLAIR, PUBLISHER
WINSTON-SALEM, NORTH CAROLINA

*The paper in this book meets the guidelines
for permanence and durability of the Committee on
Production Guidelines for Book Longevity
of the Council on Library Resources*

*Design by Debra Long Hampton
Cover image by Martin Tucker and Anne Waters*

Library of Congress Cataloging-in-Publication Data
Kirk, Stephen, 1960-
Scribblers : stalking the authors of Appalachia / by Stephen Kirk.
p.   cm.
ISBN 0-89587-307-9 (alk. paper)
1. American literature—North Carolina—Asheville Region—History and
criticism. 2. American literature—Appalachian Region,
Southern—History and criticism. 3. Authors, American—Homes and
haunts—North Carolina—Asheville Region. 4. Authors, American—Homes
and haunts—Appalachian Region, Southern. 5. Appalachian Region,
Southern—Intellectual life. 6. Appalachian Region, Southern—In
literature. 7. Asheville Region (N.C.)—Intellectual life. 8.
Asheville Region (N.C.)—In literature. I. Title.
PS266.N8K57 2004
810.9'975688—dc22
2004016038

For M, Z, and B

Contents

"Writers, like teeth, are divided into incisors and grinders."

Walter Bagehot

CHAPTER 1

Pencilneck's Holiday

The dancing Maxwell Perkins is too old for the part:
that's my first impression. The legendary Scribner's editor
was in his forties when he met Thomas Wolfe. This guy looks
a good fifteen years older.

I'm attending a ballet based on Wolfe's life. Called *A
Stone, A Leaf, A Door*, it's billed as a "world premiere." Two
of the girls in the chamber choir have barbwire tattoos
around their ankles. Stage right, a solemn-looking fellow
gravely intones poetry adapted from Wolfe while the danc-
ers emote. A stone, a leaf, and a door are the dominant symbols in *Look Homeward, Angel*. I recently finished that novel
and was hammered by those images for five hundred and
twenty-two pages. Confronting them again makes my head
hurt. Damn me for a lowbrow, but ballet seems a silly way
to tell the story. I wish I had my ten dollars back.

I've come to Asheville, North Carolina, for the Thomas

Wolfe Festival. Because of obligations at work, I was late getting on the road for the three-hour drive to this mountain city. As a result, I've missed the mock debates on the front porch of the Thomas Wolfe Memorial, the walking tour of Wolfe's Asheville, the readers' theater presentation of Wolfe's story "The Child by Tiger," the radio broadcast from the memorial, and Wolfe's posthumous birthday cake. I've missed the presentation of sundry papers—"Thomas Wolfe: A Psychobiography," "Thomas Wolfe and Aline Bernstein," "The Flood of 1916 and Thomas Wolfe's *Antaeus, or a Memory of Earth*," "Thomas Wolfe's Literary Use of the Civil War." Maybe that's for the best. To be honest, I'm not much interested anyway. And I'm too lame for the Thomas Wolfe 8K Road Race.

I don't feel much affinity for Wolfe. He was a drunk, a skirt chaser, a mama's boy, and a lout. He was needy, crude, self-pitying, and impressed with his brilliance. I admire him for his grand, naive ambition to capture the entire world on paper, but I don't much care for his writing. When I began *Look Homeward, Angel*, the book so frustrated me that I started counting all the exclamation points and penciling a running tally at the end of each chapter. "*O waste of loss, in the hot mazes, lost, among bright stars on this most weary unbright cylinder, lost!*" O juvenile crap! Like many readers before me, I later got caught up in the high madness of his thinly fictionalized family. But the novel ultimately seemed as overstated as the man himself.

Asheville impresses me as much as Thomas Wolfe doesn't. The city lies at an elevation of twenty-five hundred feet in a protected bowl of the southern Appalachians between the Blue Ridge Mountains to the east and the Great Smokies to the west. It occupies a temperate zone in which rain is more plentiful but the air is generally drier, in which the summers are cooler and the winters milder, than in the areas east and west of the mountains.

The corridor of the French Broad River first became a haven for people of means in the second quarter of the nineteenth century, when South Carolina planters seeking to escape the heat and yellow fever of the coastal lowlands built grand homes at Flat Rock, just over the North Carolina border. Meanwhile, another wealthy enclave developed at Hot Springs, fifty miles north-northwest, toward the Tennessee line. Midway between the two was Asheville, which attained a fame as "America's Magic Mountain" as the privileged escaped to its healthful climate and spectacular views.

Foremost among the Northern bluebloods who came to town was George Washington Vanderbilt, who visited with his mother in 1887. Local legend has it that Vanderbilt was on the south veranda of the Battery Park Hotel when he saw the vista of rolling mountains that inspired him to create the Biltmore Estate. Encompassing a 125,000-acre tract of forest, a 250-room chateau, and a complete support village, it was a private domain unequaled in America. Twenty-six when he began acquiring local property and thirty-three—and still a bachelor—when the chateau was completed in 1895, Vanderbilt never considered that he might have overbuilt, or that Asheville was a backwater, the railroad not having reached town until 1880. He believed that if he did things on a grand-enough scale, the world would come to him.

Aside from its beauty and climate, the area had little to recommend it. Most people were small farmers on difficult ground; they were self-sufficient but cash-strapped. The influx of wealth into what had long been a hardscrabble region brought jobs. It also furthered the tradition by which the best assets of poor places are owned by interlopers.

The juxtaposition of plenty and little was one of the factors that gave rise to a surprisingly rich writing tradition centered on a city that only recently topped fifty thousand inhabitants. Some say literacy came late here, but a rich vein of material awaited those who picked up a pen. Thomas Wolfe is Asheville's favorite son. O. Henry once had an office downtown. F. Scott Fitzgerald spent a couple of summers at the Grove Park Inn; Zelda died in an asylum fire in Asheville; Tennessee Williams organized one of his late, failed plays around that fire. Walker Percy summered for many years at nearby Highlands, where he conceived the idea for *The Second Coming*, set in Asheville. Gail Godwin spent her formative years in Asheville's Catholic schools. Charles Frazier was educated here, too; his Cold Mountain lies forty miles west. John Ehle is from West Asheville.

Draw a circle with a radius of thirty miles around the city and you take in these writers: Carl Sandburg lived out his later years in Flat Rock; Fred Chappell is from Haywood County, west of the city; Robert Morgan grew up in Henderson County, to the south; Tony Earley is from Rutherfordton, to the southeast; Lilian Jackson Braun lives half the year at Tryon, to the south; Patricia Cornwell spent part of her youth at Montreat, to the east, where she was mentored by Ruth Bell Graham, the wife of Billy Graham.

The Black Mountain College writers inhabited a strange, culturally significant little campus near Montreat.

Residing under this noble forest canopy is an understory of genre authors and writers of regional or minor national note.

Beneath that is a ground cover of writers' organizations, critique clubs, and literary retreats—the Writers' Workshop, the Asheville Plotters, the Hendersonville Writers Support Group, the Writers' Guild of Western North Carolina, the Transylvania Writers' Alliance, the Burke County Cross Country Wordsmiths, the Cashiers Writers' Group, Mountain Voices, numerous splinter groups, and, no doubt, others unknown to me.

I've traveled here to glean insights from the lives of famous authors in a town with a rich literary tradition. But more than that, I want to examine the writer's urge as manifested in flesh-and-blood scribblers, whether they be great or humble, successful or failed, recognized or frustrated. From the unknown among them, I want to learn what compels people to daily confront the limits of imagination, to continue nursing hopes when the possibility of real success is so slim. I'd like to know why writers think they can take their mostly mundane experiences and ideas and create something of value.

The final event of the Thomas Wolfe Festival is the dedication of the new visitor center at the Wolfe memorial. That facility, located behind the memorial proper—the boardinghouse known as the Old Kentucky Home in Wolfe's day and immortalized as Dixieland in *Look Homeward, Angel*—

contains restrooms, display space, a gift shop, and an auditorium. It's also designed to save wear and tear on the old boardinghouse itself.

I gather with perhaps a hundred others on the memorial's back lawn for the ceremony. In the crowd with me is Wilma Dykeman, author of *The Tall Woman* and grande dame of Appalachian literature. Among the speakers is Dr. Dietz Wolfe, a descendant of one of Thomas Wolfe's brothers. But most everyone, I suspect, has come to hear Pat Conroy.

Spiritual heir of Thomas Wolfe, Conroy shares Wolfe's verbosity and exuberance. Conroy's writing, too, has been known to ride roughshod over the family of his youth.

Ruddy, heavyset, blocklike, his hair gone nearly white, Conroy speaks of his passion for Thomas Wolfe's writing. He tells of the day when, an impressionable South Carolina high schooler, he came with his English teacher to the Thomas Wolfe Memorial. His teacher took him to the backyard where we now stand and made him eat an apple from a tree here, figuratively planting the seed of Conroy's own literary career. He has made numerous pilgrimages to Asheville since. Within the past year, he has traveled to town to write a screenplay of *Look Homeward, Angel*.

Well prepared, comfortable in front of his listeners, Conroy calls up his emotions with ease and grace.

As the gathering breaks up, I'd like to make my way to the front to meet him.

"Mr. Conroy, your speech meant a lot to me," I could say. I'm sure he's never heard that one.

Or "I love your books."

That's not exactly true. I've read only a couple, and so long ago that I'm not sure what opinion I'd hold of them today.

Or "Mr. Conroy, I have some reservations about Thomas Wolfe—and his admirers."

That would be honest, but a bad idea nonetheless, and certainly inappropriate to the occasion.

Or I could simply introduce myself.

I'm sure he'd be honored.

So I skulk away without saying anything to anyone.

The Tapestry Gallery in Biltmore House contains the estate's principal portraits. The John Singer Sargent painting of the man of the house stands out among Vanderbilt portraits because of one object in prominent view: the book in George Washington Vanderbilt's hand, held delicately at his shoulder.

The Vanderbilts were hardly bookish. George was the first intellectual in four generations of America's most acquisitive family. He began collecting books and art at age eleven and eventually amassed twenty-three thousand volumes and learned to read eight languages. His Biltmore library was a source of particular pride. The sixty-four-by-thirty-two-foot Pellegrini painting on its ceiling, disassembled from a palace in Venice, testifies to the room's size. The library holds first-class collections of history, horticulture, travel, and foreign-language titles and nineteenth-century English and American literature.

Moreover, George Vanderbilt had writerly aspirations himself. In his private study at Biltmore, which he called his "scriptorium," he penned first-person hunting adventure stories that cast him as a dashing figure in the Teddy Roosevelt mold. A couple of those stories still languish, unpublished, in a private archive.

Vanderbilt liked to host famous authors for extended stays at Biltmore.

His unhappiest guest was Henry James, then as now ignored by American readers. James came in February 1905 during his return to the United States after twenty-one years in Europe. Suffering gout, carpal tunnel syndrome that made the act of writing painful, and the aftereffects of a forty-day course of dental work, James grumbled in his correspondence that Vanderbilt's "strange, colossal heartbreaking house" was "a gorgeous practical joke."

But Edith Wharton, who arrived for the Christmas holiday that same year fresh off the publication of her breakthrough novel, *The House of Mirth*, loved the place.

One guest who is obscure today but may have cast a longer shadow than either James or Wharton in his own time was Paul Leicester Ford. In his scant thirty-seven years, Ford established a national reputation as a printer, historian, biographer, bibliographer, and novelist. His 1899 novel, *Janice Meredith: A Story of the American Revolution*, sold two hundred thousand copies in its first three months, a record to that date. One critic christened it "the great New Jersey novel," no irony intended. It spawned the Janice Meredith Waltz and a hairstyle, the "Meredith curl." The first text inside the front cover, it so happens, is a slavish page-long dedication to George Vanderbilt. "My dear George," it goes in part, "As I have read the proofs of this book I have found more than once that the pages have faded out of sight and in their stead I have seen Mount Pisgah and the French Broad River, or the ramp and terrace of Biltmore House. . . . With the visions, too, has come a recurrence to our long talks, our work among the books, our games of chess, our cups of tea, our walks, our rides, and our drives."

I saw Biltmore from the air some years ago, when I visited Asheville for a previous employer. Ignorant of where the estate lay in relation to the airport but knowing it was out there somewhere, my fellow passengers and I searched for it out the right side of the cabin as that wing lowered briefly during the climb, then swung our heads left as the aircraft banked the opposite way. Everyone let out a collective "Ah"— there it was, closer than I'd hoped, right where I might have landed at the front door had I rolled out the plane's window. It remains one of the most spectacular sights of my life.

Arriving by air is the best introduction to Asheville. Following wave upon wave of rolling green mountains, the bright downtown is a revelation. So striking is its architecture that on the heels of the city's christening as "America's Magic Mountain" came a nickname even more hifalutin: "the Paris of the South." That's too grand by a factor of twenty, but the point is taken. Instead of defaulting on its loans after the stock-market crash of 1929, Asheville made good on every cent, which meant it was still paying its Depression debt as late as 1976. The positive side of this was that the city lacked the funds or the will to remake its downtown during the urban-renewal boom. When good times returned to the area, the architectural gems of the Roaring Twenties were waiting to be dusted off.

To try to re-create my first experience of the mountains, I've booked a private tour flight. At a cost of a hundred and thirty dollars for an hour's time, it's an extravagance I can't justify. I tell myself it will clarify my purpose and give me perspective.

The office of the flight school lies at the end of a long hall in an outbuilding at Asheville's airport. One of the two men working there introduces himself as Billy and asks me what it is, exactly, I've come to see. I was vague over the phone.

"Well, is the person who'll be taking me up pretty familiar with the area? Geographically, I mean."

"All our instructors are."

"And he'll show me whatever I ask?"

"As far as he can."

I tell him I want to see Asheville proper, but also Oteen, Canton, Cold Mountain, Tryon, Hendersonville, Flat Rock, Black Mountain, Montreat, and maybe as far north as Mount Mitchell and Burnsville.

Billy takes a quick glance at his coworker. "Um, you know your hour begins as soon as the propeller starts spinning. By the time you're cleared for takeoff, then have to taxi back to the building afterwards, that's a significant amount of time right there."

I hadn't figured on that. "Of course," I say. "Obviously. Those are the places on my wish list, I mean. We'll just do the most significant. The ones we have time for, I mean."

Not everything I want to see will be as easily spotted as Biltmore—like Riverside Cemetery, which lies under tree cover on the bank of the French Broad River north of downtown. All the same, it's worth a look, as the grave of William Sydney Porter—O. Henry—lies not a hundred yards from that of Thomas Wolfe.

In 1909, warned by his New York doctor to pay attention to his failing health, O. Henry came south to stay with the family of his wife, Sara Lindsay Coleman, an Asheville native.

After examining America's most popular story writer, a local physician diagnosed him as having high blood pressure and an enlarged heart and liver, along with mental and nervous exhaustion, all of which he ascribed to alcoholism.

"Mr. Porter, how many drinks do you take in a day?" the doctor asked.

"Oh, four or five," the author conservatively estimated.

"When do you take the first one?"

"When I first get up."

"The next one?"

"Well, sometimes that does not seem to take hold, and I take another while I'm shaving."

O. Henry began a program of exercise and may have forsworn alcohol for the first time in many years. His health responded.

His stay in Asheville had another purpose, too. Jack London had recently made the transition from short-story writer to novelist, and O. Henry planned to do the same. He took an office on the fifth floor of Asheville's American National Bank Building, where he spent hours looking out his window at the people in the streets. Among the passersby was undoubtedly the young Thomas Wolfe, nine years old and with hair cascading below his shoulders.

The novel form proved hopelessly daunting. O. Henry's preference was to write a complete piece at a single sitting, a habit that served him ill now. And the public loved him for his light, quick, clever, formulaic stories, not the kind of serious, deeply personal narrative he had in mind.

The pull of the big city was irresistible. His final word on Asheville? "There was too much scenery and fresh air. What I need is a steam-heated flat with no ventilation or exercise." His only literary production during his time in the mountains was "Let Me Feel Your Pulse," an unfunny humorous story that sought to make light of his alcoholism and other health problems. He returned to New York to try to adapt some of his stories for Broadway. He resumed his old habits and died within five months, at age forty-seven.

A short hop east from Riverside Cemetery is the Grove Park Inn, which lies atop Sunset Mountain within the city. I'll have no trouble spotting its famous orange roof from the air.

In early 1935, F. Scott Fitzgerald left Baltimore for Asheville when he learned that his tuberculosis, long inactive, was beginning to damage his lungs. Not wanting word of his disease to harm his publishing prospects, he didn't check into a clinic but rather took up residence at the Grove Park Inn, an exclusive resort well beyond his means, and placed himself under the care of a local specialist.

He had previously mentioned Asheville in his fiction. It was the hometown of Monsignor Darcy, Amory Blaine's confessor in *This Side of Paradise*. Fitzgerald, a master stylist but no spelling-bee champ, wrote it as both *Ashville* and

Asheville in the same paragraph. The book is still printed that way today.

An icon to the previous generation, Fitzgerald was being forgotten by the present one. Sales of *Tender Is the Night*, published in 1934, were disappointing. *Taps at Reveille*, his 1935 short-story collection, was doing worse yet. The stories he wrote that year—among them one narrated by a dog—brought little money. He was on the wagon, which for Fitzgerald meant forsaking gin and drinking beer instead, as many as thirty-five bottles per day. He took sleeping pills to go to bed at night and Benzedrine to get up in the morning.

He still had his charm and his delicate good looks, though. He began simultaneous affairs with a local prostitute and a young, married, wealthy Texan staying at the inn.

When the married woman's husband arrived in North Carolina, Fitzgerald felt the urge to seek new lodgings. The first place he tried was the Old Kentucky Home, still operated as a boardinghouse by Julia Wolfe, Thomas Wolfe's mother. In a gregarious mood, Mrs. Wolfe showed him around the place and spoke at length of her famous son. It was only after they were back on the porch that she noticed Fitzgerald's tipsy state. "I never take drunks—not if I know it," she said. She stepped inside and slammed the screen behind her.

Fitzgerald left North Carolina late that summer. He was back the following April, when he transferred Zelda from an asylum in New York to Asheville's Highland Hospital and resumed his residence at the Grove Park Inn. That July, Scott took her swimming at nearby Lake Lure. In performing a swan dive off a fifteen-foot board, he broke his shoulder. Fitzgerald was placed in a body cast with his right arm elevated, after which he had to dictate what little writing he did.

In September, a reporter from the *New York Post* traveled to the Grove Park Inn to profile Fitzgerald on his fortieth birthday. The front-page article born of that interview described Fitzgerald as a despairing drunk who wore the "pitiful expression of a cruelly beaten child," who "stumbled over to the highboy [to pour] himself another drink." Upon reading the piece, Fitzgerald attempted to kill himself by ingesting an overdose of morphine, which he vomited up. When he fired a revolver during a subsequent suicide threat, the management refused to let him remain at the inn unless he kept a nurse in attendance.

Several Scribner's authors sought to aid him during his dark days. Ernest Hemingway headed north for Asheville from Key West but had to change his plans. Marjorie Kinnan Rawlings, holed up at Banner Elk in the North Carolina mountains while she wrote *The Yearling*, visited Fitzgerald in the fall of 1936. At lunch, Fitzgerald started with a bottle of white wine and one of sherry, then ordered "a bottle of port, and as the afternoon wore on, another and another," according to Rawlings.

Most significantly, Thomas Wolfe came in May 1937. The two authors met in nearby Tryon, where Fitzgerald was temporarily staying. They discussed *Gone With the Wind*, which Wolfe pronounced "too damn long"—an odd criticism from a man of his verbiage.

"Tom," Fitzgerald asked as they were preparing to part company, "how old are you now?"

"Why, Scott, I'll soon be thirty-seven."

"My God, Tom. I'm forty. Look, bud, we're at a dangerous age. You know in this country we burn ourselves out at the work we are doing, and this is particularly true of writers."

It was seven and a half years since Wolfe had been home. This was his long-delayed return following the publication of *Look Homeward, Angel*, in which he skewered the mountain town of Altamont—a thinly fictionalized Asheville—telling of its drunks, mulattos, illegitimate children, and prostitutes; exposing hatred and prejudice; and creating a sexual undercurrent that was very frank for its time.

Look Homeward, Angel was released at the unluckiest time imaginable—on October 18, 1929, five days before the stock-market crash—but Wolfe overpowered that misfortune with the sweep of his prose. In Asheville, the $2.50 novel rented for $.50 per day. Some local residents were amused to see their neighbors' follies in print; a few were flattered by Wolfe's portrayal of themselves; most were outraged. The local public library didn't shelve the book until 1935, when Scott Fitzgerald, during his first summer in town, purchased two copies, brought them to the library, plunked them down on the desk, and asked that they be put in circulation.

So it was that Wolfe had mixed feelings about coming home after the novel's publication.

His reception proved surprisingly warm. People had bigger concerns than bearing an old grudge. Welcomed as a local boy who'd made good, Wolfe walked his old newspaper route, addressed a local business club, and contributed an article to the paper. Pleased at the attention, he arranged to rent a secluded cabin in Oteen, just east of Asheville, where he did some writing that July.

A famous letter exchange came out of the meeting between the two great authors in little Tryon. Fitzgerald wrote Wolfe at the cabin in Oteen urging him to stifle his desire to produce expansive books, but rather, like Scott himself, to try a "novel of selected incidents."

"Don't forget, Scott, that a great writer is not only a leaver-outer but also a putter-inner," Wolfe replied, "and that Shakespeare and Cervantes and Dostoievsky were great putter-inners—greater putter-inners, in fact, than taker-outers."

Fitzgerald departed the Asheville area in late June or early July 1937. Wolfe left on September 2. Neither ever returned. Wolfe died one year later and Fitzgerald three.

There seems to be a problem with my flight.

"Um, your pilot had a dead battery in his car this morning," Billy says after some hesitation.

"But he's here now?"

"Well, his car was towed. He called in. He's still at the garage."

This sounds suspicious. It's now midafternoon. My missing pilot has had plenty of time to get his battery recharged or replaced.

"Um, they must have found something else wrong," Billy ventures.

"So what should I do? Is someone filling in for him?"

"No, but . . . Here, I'll show you."

I follow him down the hall to a lounge that looks out on a loading area, taxiway, and runway. Not ten yards from the window, a teenage boy and a man of about thirty are climbing into a red prop plane.

"Charlie's headed out on a lesson. If he's done by four, maybe he can take you up. Otherwise, we're booked the rest of the day."

If it proves necessary, I can skip most of the outlying sites. But Connemara, the big, old house on Little Grassy Mountain, remains a must-see.

It was 1945 when Carl Sandburg bought Connemara and its two hundred forty-five acres at Flat Rock. "What a hell of a baronial estate for an old Socialist like me!" he said. He relished the irony that the biographer of Lincoln should spend his declining years in a home that once belonged to Christopher Memminger, the first secretary of the Confederate treasury.

Then in his sixties, Sandburg was thought to have little left to say. Once considered the heir to Walt Whitman, he had seen his poetic style go out of vogue soon after it came in. His sprawling biography of Lincoln won him a Pulitzer but was more remarkable for its enthusiasm than its scholarship. "The cruelest thing that has happened to Lincoln since he was shot by Booth has been to fall into the hands of Carl Sandburg," wrote one critic. Poets considered him a good biographer, while biographers judged him a fair poet.

And now he was selling out to the movies. When he arrived at Connemara, Sandburg was deep into an MGM-commissioned novel that the studio hoped to turn into an epic patriotic film. Seventy-five thousand words were what MGM was after, but Sandburg was already up to four hundred thousand, and the end was nowhere in sight. Alone in his third-floor writer's nest, wearing a shade when his overworked eyes troubled him, which was often, he customarily worked through the night and into the early morning.

As Sandburg was wrestling with his novel, the colony of artists at nearby Black Mountain College was undergoing a crisis of identity. I'd like to see the college's two former campuses, both of which ought to be visible from the air.

I watch the airport traffic while I wait in the lounge. Billy takes good care of me, coming back down the hall a couple of times to make sure I'm comfortable, apologizing for my pilot's absence, pouring me cups of coffee I don't want but drink anyway, chatting about the new aircraft the school is to receive next week.

Black Mountain was a Euro-Yankee experiment in the Southern highlands, the majority of its faculty being from abroad and its student body from the Northeast. People at the college wanted nothing to do with hillbillies. And the school's willful isolation was fine with the locals, who saw the place as a haven for free love, godlessness, homosexuals, and egotists.

For a college in the middle of nowhere that teetered on the brink of financial ruin, that existed for only twenty-three years, and whose enrollment never reached a hundred students, Black Mountain attracted a remarkable collection of talent. Its instructors included Buckminster Fuller, John Cage, Robert Rauschenberg, and Merce Cunningham. Among its visitors were Albert Einstein, Thornton Wilder, Henry Miller, Aldous Huxley, Zora Hurston, and Langston Hughes.

When enrollment dipped to two dozen in the early 1950s,

faculty and students hit upon the idea of creating a magazine as a means of publicizing the college. The *Black Mountain Review* started out small and ingrown, pieces by instructors Charles Olson and Robert Creeley front and center.

Even as the student body fell to single digits and it grew obvious the college was a lost cause, the magazine took flight. Carl Jung and Jorge Luis Borges submitted material. *Black Mountain Review #7*, the final issue, ran well over two hundred pages and included original pieces by Allen Ginsberg and Jack Kerouac and sections from William S. Burroughs's unpublished *Naked Lunch*. By the time it came out in the fall of 1957, the college had disbanded.

A mix of poetry, short fiction, criticism, essays, letters, and photography, the *Review* was one of only a handful of print outlets—and probably the premier forum—for avant-garde artists in the political climate of the mid-1950s. Its influence on the next generation of writers was considerable. It is still admired today.

Carl Sandburg and the college, though neighbors, found little common ground.

"Where is the Sandburg who talked of picket lines?" Black Mountain poet Kenneth Rexroth asked. "Where is the Sandburg who sang of whores?"

"I am not going to talk about whores at my age," Sandburg remarked upon hearing Rexroth's queries.

But radicals come in different stripes.

Sandburg's MGM-contracted novel weighed in at over a thousand printed pages. An attempt to encompass the entire American experience, it spanned the years from the Pilgrims through World War II. He called it *Remembrance*

Rock. It was a critical failure lambasted for its clunky structure, its tangle of subplots, and its woodenly allegorical characters. "As dull and tedious a literary performance as has been foisted on the public in many months," one reviewer wrote. "An amazing exhibition of how not to write a novel." Commissioned for screen adaptation, it was entirely unusable for that purpose.

Yet there is something heroic about a man with little to gain and much to risk who tackled a new form in his late sixties and tried to write something for the ages.

Still energetic in his seventies, Sandburg published his *Complete Poems*, which won him a second Pulitzer; wrote the autobiography of his early years; condensed his Lincoln opus into a single-volume edition; and wrote the prologue for *The Family of Man*, Edward Steichen's landmark photographic collection. A man of humble origin who considered himself poor even when he was rich, Sandburg grabbed whatever financial opportunities came his way, intent on building an inheritance for his two invalid daughters, one of whom was epileptic and the other of whom was hit by a car when she was sixteen, suffered a fractured skull, and lived the rest of her life on the level of a twelve-year-old.

But what really moved him was a lifelong desire to teach himself how to write. "Before you go to sleep at night, you say, 'I haven't got it yet. I haven't got it yet,' " he once remarked.

Billy is standing with me at the window when he spies the little red plane off in the distance to our right. "Just on time," he says.

It's a moment before I spot it; looked at edge-on, it's

like trying to see a knife in the sky. The plane comes in right wing low but finally straightens when it's just beyond the edge of the runway and maybe fifty feet off the ground. Unlike the jets that rumble the windows of the lounge, the little red plane is completely silent to us. It touches down opposite where we're standing, then lifts back up, climbs, and starts to bank left past the far end of the runway.

Billy taps his foot three, four, five times before he speaks. "Touch-and-go's," he says.

"What?"

"They're doing touch-and-go's. The student must have the plane till five."

"Oh."

"We can fit you in tomorrow, no problem."

"But I live out of town. I'm heading home tonight."

And so I do, but not before Billy pours and caps me a coffee for the road, walks me to the parking lot, and elicits my promise to contact the flight school when I'm coming to the mountains again.

I doubt I'll take him up on his offer.

I doubt he means it anyway.

It's hardly his fault my trip has been a failure. A hundred-and-thirty-dollar flight probably wasn't going to buy me much understanding anyway. What I really need to do is meet some actual writers.

CHAPTER 2

Authors Anonymous

When you write a book, you expect it to impact the world in some small way, though you ought to know better. If you hope to see your achievement celebrated and instead find yourself a lonely supplicant, it is profoundly discouraging.

My first book came out some years ago.

I've never happened across anyone reading it on the beach, on an airplane, or in a library.

I've never witnessed anyone buying it in a bookstore except at my autographings.

I've watched boxes of my book leave the publisher's warehouse in October and return unopened after the holidays. I've seen individual copies trickle back unsold, be-stickered, and battered.

I've been politely declined when I offered to speak about being an author to my daughter's fourth-grade class.

At one autographing, I had a group of children feel sorry enough that they pooled their resources and bought post-cards for me to sign, since they couldn't afford the price of a book, intended for adult readers anyway.

Eighteen months after publication, bookstore returns of unsold copies were so strong that I received a semiannual royalty check for exactly $1.01, meaning that, over the preceding six months, sales had exceeded returns by exactly one unit. I never cashed that check. I have it still.

But I say it's a pretty good book nonetheless. And I shouldn't disparage its sales. It's been through three printings and one foreign-language edition and remains a staple in its niche nearly a decade after publication.

When the book-writing spirit again moves me, I decide to take as my subject mountain writers, from the iconic to the unknown. I return to Asheville several weeks after the Thomas Wolfe Festival to seek out a local writers' support group. The largest such organization in the area is The Writers' Workshop. On its advisory board, I see from its professional-looking newsletter, are such luminaries as John Le Carré, Peter Matthiessen, and Reynolds Price. Oddly, Alex Haley is listed as a member of the board—at the bottom and in smaller type—though it is years since his death; someone from the workshop apparently took pains to cultivate his acquaintance and will be damned if they'll let him out of a commitment. The Writers' Workshop offers seminars for beginning writers, children's writers, screenwriters, short-fiction writers, teenage writers, and single writers. It sponsors a short-story contest with a first prize of six hundred dollars—good money for that sort of thing.

When I see that the workshop is putting together a new critique group, I arrange to take half a day off work to attend the organizational meeting. It is my first long venture from home since replacing my car's water pump, so I keep an eye on the temperature gauge on the hard slog up the mountains. But it isn't until I'm idling College, Patton, and the other downtown streets futilely looking for a parking spot that the needle starts rising. I leave my car in the deck behind the civic center and walk.

Downtown Asheville provides a colorful contrast to the traditional, conservative values of the high country. Those expecting the Bible Belt are in for a funky surprise.

This area of the mountains has been a spiritual center since the time of the Cherokees. Asheville sits atop America's most powerful vortex—this according to metaphysical author Page Bryant and local swami Nostradamus Virato. Vortexes are bioelectric energy points spread across the globe like acupuncture points on the human body. A vortex occurs at the junction of "ley lines" on the earth's surface. Twenty-four vortexes have been identified between Black Mountain, to the east, and Waynesville, to the west. A vortex is a place of high energy in a small geographical area, whereas a "power spot" is the site of a lesser concentration of energy in a larger space. Mount Pisgah is the area's principal power spot. As such, it is home to Asheville's "Watcher," or guardian angel. How all of this came about is not entirely certain. Some say the quartz-filled mountains exert a "piezoelectric effect." Others maintain the area is blessed because the people of Atlantis settled here upon evacuating their dying continent.

You'll hear a lot of this kind of stuff when you come downtown.

New Agers flock to Asheville like conventioneers to a titty bar. The town has been called "a City of Light for the New Millennium," "the San Francisco of the South," and "America's New Age Mecca." In attitude, it is said to be kin to places like Sedona, Arizona; Santa Cruz and Marin County, California; Boulder, Colorado; Maui, Hawaii; and Seattle, Washington. Its downtown is the province of hopheads and health-food mavens, pamphleteers and tattoo freaks, ponytailed men and hairy-legged women, lost souls and Chosen.

Since I'm early for my meeting, I duck into Malaprop's, Asheville's noted independent bookstore. The place captures the town's contrasts pretty succinctly.

Malaprop's is one of the stores credited with pushing *Cold Mountain* early on and helping to launch that book's great run. At the front, looking out on Haywood Street, is a stained-glass commemorative window bearing the facial likenesses of some of the area's signature authors—Thomas Wolfe, Gail Godwin, Robert Morgan, Fred Chappell, John Ehle, Wilma Dykeman, and mystery writer Elizabeth Daniels Squire.

At the table by the window, bathed in its colored glow, sit a heavyset, fiftyish woman in boots and a jean jacket and a delicate girl of about twenty with at least a dozen piercings in her ear. They hold hands and speak intimately.

In the corridor leading to the bathrooms is a bulletin board crowded with brochures for Kirtan devotional chanting, multifaith healing services, bliss gatherings, drumming workshops, Zen Shiatsu Asian Bodywork, Capoeira Angola Afro-Brazilian Martial Arts, and other things incomprehensible to me.

The bookstore shelves bear such labels as "Lesbian Fiction," "Gay Fiction," "Gay and Lesbian Nonfiction," "Goddess," "Channeling," "Shamanism," "Mind-Altering Drugs," "Pagan," and "Crystals/Alien."

At a small desk about halfway to the back of the store is today's featured writer, a children's author who has come to autograph copies of his book. He tinkers with the boom box he brought with him, which begins to play what I take to be a recording of him reading his book. That technique will guarantee his isolation, I'm afraid.

On my way out, I stop by the racks of free magazines to collect some samples. These aren't real-estate guides and used-car locators. I take copies of *Spirit in the Smokies* ("A magazine of New Paradigm Living"); *Asheville Global Report*, an anti-law-enforcement rant; *Critter* ("Animal adoption and education in Asheville, Buncombe, Madison, Henderson and Haywood Counties"); *Eco Voyager* ("Changing the world one community at a time"); *New Life Journal* ("Healing & whole foods in the Appalachians"); *Southern Voice*, a gay and lesbian publication; *Community Connections* ("Serving Western North Carolina's lesbian, gay, bisexual and transgendered community"); *Forest Advocate; Wild Mountain Times* ("A journal of the Southern Appalachian Biodiversity Project"); and *Creations* ("Inspiring the soul thru healing, creativity & down-to-earth spirituality").

Half a block from the store, a Jesus-looking young man

tries to stop passersby. He eyeballs me, hesitates, but then sees the publications I'm carrying.

"You look like a pretty open-minded person. Cool," he says.

I'm the farthest thing from cool, as we both can plainly see. Besides, I don't respond well to flattery.

He lives on a ten-acre commune with twenty other people, he tells me—or maybe it's a twenty-acre commune with ten other people. They've built their own shelter from scraps and are trying to raise their own food. At his feet is a stack of comic books, one of which he offers me now.

He and his mates are selling the comics to help support themselves. Any donation, he says, will help them in their effort toward "building a society that doesn't suck."

I wish him luck in that. "But I just got all of these magazines for free," I say.

The Writers' Workshop is headquartered in the Flatiron Building on Battery Park Avenue, an eight-story version of the New York landmark. I am the second person to arrive. The offices are on the third floor. The door is locked, so I sit in the hallway on a padded bench opposite four or five folding chairs.

Over the next thirty minutes, I see why the workshop has so much seating outside its door. Enough would-be critique-group members show up to fill the available space, but no one from the organization comes to let us in. Among my new friends are a woman freelance writer and editor who has recently moved to the area from Atlanta and a pair of lovebirds who sit too close together and will be all over each other the first chance they get. The girl says she sells vacuum cleaners door to door, a line of work I thought passed from existence decades ago.

We tell each other what kind of material we write. Though we've all come to join a critique group and don't require the workshop's blessing to go ahead and inaugurate one now, no one takes the initiative. In fact, I sense a general relief that such a group will not come to pass. As we say our good-byes, the young lady prevails upon the freelancer to review a portion of her novel-in-progress. Almost as an afterthought, the freelancer volunteers that she belongs to a smaller writers' group that meets at a branch of the local library on the second Saturday of each month. When I express interest, she takes my name and address and promises to send me directions to the library.

I have no real expectation of hearing from her, but a letter arrives within a couple of days.

My first impression of the writers' group—uncharitable, I admit—is of age. Liver-spotted skin here, a worn-out hip and a bad limp there. Gnarled hands, stooped backs. Once I pay the group's yearly fee, I become the junior member by ten or twelve years, and I stand a good quarter-century below the average age. This is one of those associations where people gather to applaud each other's unpublished poetry, for the privilege of having their own praised in its turn.

They are pleased to have me, especially when they learn I am an actual full-time editor for an actual publishing company. Despite my saying that I come as a fellow writer, and not in any official capacity, they seem to believe I'm a talent scout looking for material. Any questions about publishing are referred to me. When they take me at my word on matters as diverse as contracts, distribution, and design, all of which are outside my expertise, it confirms my opinion that they're amateurs.

Actually, I misjudge them on all counts.

I understand this when it comes time to put some of my own material on the line. The members are intimately familiar with each other's writing; they exchange manuscripts individually and read poems, stories, and essays aloud to the group. By contrast, I am rather cryptic about the book I'm planning and about why I feel a need to travel a hundred and fifty miles to the Asheville area to participate in a writers' group. Though they never push me, I sense that I should either offer something of my own for public consumption or explain myself in greater detail.

My choice is an old piece of fiction that has been sitting in a drawer for years. Alone among my stories, it still gives me pleasure.

When I was twenty-two and taking a fiction-writing seminar in graduate school, I wrote a story that was recommended by my professor for publication in the literary magazine put out by my university. From there, it was selected by the great John Updike for reprinting in the *Best American Short Stories* series—all without my having put it in the mail anywhere. That was my first publication, and it remains the greatest stroke of luck of my life.

But I like the story I bring to the writers' group better. It concerns a man who, having lost an arm in an accident, resumes his avocation of refereeing high-school basketball games. Not fully recovered from his injury and out of practice, he makes a couple of bad calls against the home team, but the crowd members—many of whom know of his troubles—greet him with scattered words of encouragement rather than boos. Strangely, this provokes him to call fouls on the team's star player. Though they're beginning to get heated, the local folks continue to restrain themselves. Finally, on an inbounds play where the home cheerleaders are stationed, one of the young ladies leans into his ear and makes a quiet comment that turns him red—and starts him on his recovery.

The story brought me the finest rejection letter I've ever gotten. "Everyone here who read this found it a funny, accurate, and beautifully developed little study in psychology," an editor at *The New Yorker* wrote me. She generously suggested I try the *Atlantic, Esquire,* and *GQ.*

I chose instead to revise the story a year later and mail it back to *The New Yorker,* at which time I received a form rejection with a handwritten postscript that my editor friend was no longer with the magazine. As is my custom, I left the story to molder after that.

But now, for the benefit of my writers' group, I tighten it by three pages, eliminate an extraneous character, and change the title. It is leaner and faster than what I sent *The New Yorker*—and a good bit better than anything I've heard at our monthly meetings, in my estimation. I make fifteen photocopies for the benefit of anyone who'd like to examine it more closely after my reading.

The story begins with the referee's shoe coming untied. His partner, thinking he's doing a favor, halts the action while the accident victim goes to one knee and tries to fix his lace. It's a newly learned skill, and a difficult one, and he's having to perform it under pressure in the most public of settings.

I'm barely done describing how to tie a shoelace with one hand and giving the background on his accident when I'm interrupted.

"Thank you, Steve. That's a good story."

"Shall I continue reading?" I've barely finished three pages. I have fifteen to go.

"No, I think we have a couple of others who've brought material today." This is the group's director. "Thanks for sharing it with us, though." Then, turning to the members, he says, "Does anyone want to comment?"

"It's a very good story. I enjoyed it," someone says.

"Yes."

"I agree."

There is a pause.

"It gets started kind of slowly," someone offers.

"It does begin slowly."

"With today's readers, you've got to hook them early."

"If you don't grab them in the first page, they'll move on to something else."

"There are demands on everybody's lives. You've got to get their attention."

"Don't bore people. Don't waste their time."

"You ought to take your main action and move it up front."

The director thanks me again for sharing.

"The writing really is beautiful," someone says.

"I agree."

"Bring it back when you revise it. We'd love to hear it again."

I carry my fifteen copies home.

One interesting thing about the members is their simultaneous love of books and hatred of mainstream publishing. Fortunately, their feelings don't extend to me as a representative of the industry, but neither do they strive to hide them in my presence. These are people who feel they've been wronged. They've been belittled, bilked, screwed, and shat upon by editors, agents, get-published-quick scams, magazines, book publishers, contest chairmen, and assorted others. A few have achieved modest success, but none has reached the plateau to which they'd like to ascend, and the shortsightedness, the lack of imagination, the greed, and the herd mentality of publishing people are held to be at fault for that.

Bitter though they are, and grouse though they certainly do, they'll never stop reaching for the prize. They've all been deeply touched by books. They'll keep attending conferences, exchanging manuscripts, corresponding with kindred spirits, entering contests, subscribing to writers' magazines, introducing themselves to booksellers, hobnobbing with insiders, reading the classics, researching the market, looking for an angle, practicing their craft, submitting their work, and consoling each other as long as they draw breath. This at an age when most of their peers are enjoying their ease.

Frankie Schelly writes social-issues novels that fare well in the various contests in which she enters them. But when it comes to publication, her tale is one of unleavened frustration. She wants commercial success and refuses to lower her sights. At meetings, her talk is always of hiring and firing agents, a cycle of expectations raised and then dashed.

Steve Brown gave up his job in the prime of life to write full-time. He doesn't know how he'll face his kids if he doesn't find success, after they've seen him put himself in a position of dependency. He confesses to me that he wouldn't even have a car to drive if his mother-in-law hadn't leased him one. He runs up quite a tab, too, joining writers' organizations, attending conferences out of state, and establishing acquaintanceships with editors and agents. He has a series of four mysteries with a Generation X female protagonist, as well as a couple of mainstream novels, but no publications, and little promise of any.

Jack Pyle and his good friend Taylor Reese have cowritten a couple of gardening books for a small commercial publisher, which they sell out of the trunks of their cars. They are regular speakers at bookstores, garden shops, and library gatherings through parts of four states.

These are a few of my new friends. Privately, I hold myself superior, since my idea is so much better than any of theirs. It's axiomatic that a writer judges his peers by what they have in print and himself by the stories playing in his head, which are of a higher realm than anything he'll ever get on paper.

There's a portion of my house where, to get up under the eaves to paint, I have to tilt the ladder at an uncomfortably low angle, so my head is only about a foot higher than my knees. And the sideways slope of the land is such that I can't even the ladder by laying a board under the lower side. Rather, I have to put a thick board under the lower end and a thinner one on the high side.

Anyway, I am precariously in the air painting as quickly as I can when I feel the feet of the ladder start to slip backwards off the boards. Suddenly, I am riding the top of the ladder down the side of the house. There is nothing to grab onto and nowhere to jump. I steel myself to land chest-first on the heat pump from a height of ten or twelve feet. I don't know if I holler or not.

I am saved when the ladder's feet slide all the way off the boards and dig into the turf and stop. The only harm is a couple of furrows in the lawn and matching scratches down the side of the house. There is nothing to do but adjourn inside for a drink and a towel, try to set the ladder more firmly, and have at it once more.

I'm not fond of symbols and metaphors and seldom understand or even recognize them when I see them. But I know my major preparation for writing a new book to be a symbolic act.

The spring before I started my first book, it so happened that our house needed painting and we didn't have the money to hire someone to do it. In accordance with my practice of always doing things the hardest way possible, I spent my spare moments from May through October—nights, weekends, days off—first scrubbing the boards clean with a bathroom brush and a bucket of bleach mixed half and half with water, then painting the whole thing with a three-inch brush, or rather several of them in turn as they wore out or gummed up and stiffened. At first, I understood no connection between that labor and my writing, but I gradually came to see it as steeling myself for the long, solitary desk work ahead.

Painting the house that summer remains the hardest physical labor I've ever done. The ridiculousness of my method drew a few comments from neighbors, and I couldn't disagree with them. Then again, I knew that I'd get a book written and they never would.

Now, eight years later, the place wants paint again. Our finances are in better shape, yet I feel a need to readdress my fears—to be standing twenty feet off the ground worried about bees flying up my shirt, and then to do it again the next weekend, and the next, until the job is done.

Like writing, painting puts me in a foul mood. I like people to offer their help, though I don't really want it. I'm open to suggestions, though I won't do the work any way other than what I've planned. I remain a family man, though the job will be done when it needs to be done and take as long as it takes and have priority over everything else.

My parents are after me all summer to let them lend a hand. I try to explain that the work is proceeding on schedule, that it's a hot, nasty job, and that they're welcome to come and play with the kids but would be unwise to paint with me. I even warn them that they might find me in ill spirits. They come anyway, early one Sunday afternoon.

On Sunday afternoons during painting, I tend to be mad because I've spent the coolest part of the day at church, only to have sweat running into my eyes by the time I get the ladder set up and the bucket stirred. I'm madder this day, since it's mid-August and I'm working on the south side of the house.

"You know, it's a lot cooler around back," my father says. "It'll be like trying to spread tar here in front."

I explain that I intend to finish each side of the house before moving on to the next, even if that makes me the stupidest man alive. I don't care how hot it is, I don't want the place looking like a patchwork quilt. As regards the present day's labor, I told them in advance that I've already done the picture window and the front wall as far as the door, and that if they want to come and help, the south side of the house is what will be painted today.

"Your main concern should be your health," my mother says. "You can always work on this side after supper."

"I'm going around back," my father says.

My mother keeps badgering me about finding her something to paint—preferably in back. She also wants me to be sure to "hydrate." She tells me this often.

"Dammit, Mom, I'm thirty-eight years old. I know how to hydrate," I finally tell her. My father has come around the house and is looking at me as I say this. I try to talk nicer. "If you really want to do something, take the kids to the pool."

But she prefers to work, so I get down off the ladder to find her a bucket and brush.

Seeing her mother-in-law painting, my wife suddenly has to help, too. This is the first time all summer she's shown the inclination.

Meanwhile, the kids are unsupervised and tearing up the house. I can hear them yelling and pounding across the floor. It's very distressing how things are getting so far out of my control.

"Could someone please take the kids to the pool?" I ask.

Five minutes later, I'm in my swim trunks and sandals and shepherding my daughters to the car myself. Let the others paint the whole damn house if they want.

But being a decent son at my core, I come back and apologize. My parents have driven a hundred miles, after all, and will have to travel home later, after being out in the sun.

As it turns out, my mother doesn't make it beyond twenty minutes. Her face flushes in the heat and her hands start trembling, so she leaves her brush and goes inside. My father soon follows, and then my wife, which lets me return to doing things the way I like.

No more ill words are exchanged on the subject, and any sour feelings pass quickly. But I notice that I'm thereafter left alone with brush, paint, and a big, bare wall against which to test myself.

CHAPTER 3

Big Game

It's easy to gain the confidence of unpublished and small-time writers. They crave attention but haven't received much of it. They'll latch onto anything they think might elevate their status or give them a forum to express their views. I know this because I am one of the tribe.

For the purposes of my own book-to-be, though, I understand from an early stage that I must have some name-brand authors on board. I need to bask in their reflected glow. I want to know whether Thomas Wolfe's town has had an influence on their careers. I'd like to learn what training and what writerly habits have contributed to their success. I don't want to dwell on their best work but to learn what they're doing in the here and now, when their paths cross mine. One of my fondest hopes is that, if I ingratiate myself well enough, one or two will let me eavesdrop on their creative process as they write their next book. If and when it comes time for me to seek a publisher, their presence in my manuscript will lend it legitimacy.

I'm unsure where to start.

Charles Frazier is probably the biggest fish in the pond, but I want to have commitments from other authors before I try to approach him.

I've never met Robert Morgan, but my company published the paperback edition of his first novel, so I have a means of introduction. Still, he teaches at Cornell now, five states away, and I'd rather begin with some face-to-face interviews.

John Ehle lives close to where I do. But I'm told he's in delicate health, having suffered from Parkinson's for many years.

I get the impression Lilian Jackson Braun is reclusive.

I understand Patricia Cornwell is a handful.

Unbeknownst to her, Gail Godwin becomes my choice for my book's first interview.

This is largely a matter of convenience. Godwin is giving a reading at the women's college in the city where I live. The next day, she will be in Asheville autographing at Malaprop's. That works perfectly for me, since I've planned a research trip to the mountains that day anyway. I'll let her audition for me at the women's college, after which I'll introduce myself at Malaprop's and lay the groundwork for an interview in the near future. She lives in New York State now, but she has a condominium in Asheville and visits in the spring and fall. When she's in town, she takes tea and a *New York Times* on the porch at the Grove Park Inn. That would be a good place for us to get together. True, *A Southern Family* is the only novel of hers I've read. But I can brush up on her canon between now and the interview. I realize this is probably a half-assed way to prepare, but I'm not writing a dissertation on her, after all.

I bring one of my daughters with me to Godwin's reading. We arrive a few minutes early, but the lecture hall is already so crowded that we are forced to sit in the back row near the door, as others in search of seats stream in behind us. A representative of the college soon steps to the stage and informs us that, in view of the audience size, the event will be moved to the larger auditorium across the hall. My daughter is out the door like she's spring-loaded. The first one in the other auditorium, she descends all the way to the front and sits in the middle of the first row. Our vantage point couldn't be better.

Gail Godwin is a gracious, deep-thinking, soft-spoken woman. She goes out of her way to compliment the intelligence of the young women of the college she lunched with earlier in the day. Her reading is well delivered but has a religious bent to it, which sets my mind to wandering. My daughter's preference is stories about animals, so the reading holds limited interest for her, too, though she is impressed when I tell her I'll be interviewing Godwin.

It doesn't work out quite that way.

I pick up a copy of Godwin's latest book at Malaprop's the next day. As I stand in the autograph line, my conviction begins to wilt, the thinness of my justification for requesting an interview just now hitting home.

Maybe bluster can carry the day. I step up to the table,

my name and qualifications on the tip of my tongue. Godwin looks up at me briefly, then looks up again, quicker this time.

Is it fear I read in her face? She's an observant woman; she's not a famous author for nothing. She saw me in the audience a hundred and fifty miles away just last night, sitting in the front row, large as life. She must think I'm a stalker.

Perhaps the interview should wait until later. I ask her to sign the book to my daughter, after which I depart the store quietly.

I'll have better luck with Sharyn McCrumb.

I'm acquainted with a librarian who worked with her on a newspaper years ago. The president of the company where I'm employed is a friend of Sharyn's who helped her with research on *The Ballad of Frankie Silver*. I once had dinner with Sharyn and several other admirers before one of Sharyn's local autographings, though she may not remember me.

If my Asheville friends can be said to have a patron saint, it is Sharyn McCrumb. Through fourteen or so novels and—at last count—two *New York Times* bestsellers, an Anthony Award, an Agatha Award, two Macavity Awards, a Nero Award, two *Los Angeles Times* Notable Books, and three *New York Times* Notable Books, she hasn't forgotten that she, too, was once a writers' group regular with big plans but little to show for them. My friends admire her because she always has time for people who take the craft of writing seriously—whether they're successful or not—and also because she doesn't suffer fools. Whenever someone tries to insinuate himself into the brotherhood by saying, "I plan to sit down and write a novel someday," she comes back with something like this: "And I want to learn to be a brain surgeon, when I can find the time."

If you want a copy of a new Sharyn McCrumb book in western North Carolina, you'd better reserve it in advance or be on hand when the store unpacks the boxes, else you'll have to wait until it's back in stock. People appreciate her concern for Appalachian issues and her reverence for mountain history.

Jack Pyle and Taylor Reese from my writers' group have known her for ten years or more. In fact, they're fictionalized as environmental commandos in *The Hangman's Beautiful Daughter*, the second of Sharyn's Appalachian Ballad novels. In that book, two boyhood friends are reunited as old men. Soon after they renew their friendship, one of them is discovered to have liver cancer. "I'm the sick one," Taylor says. The incidence of cancer is uncommonly high along the river where Taylor's character lives, and a paper mill that discharges chemicals upstream is very likely the culprit. As Taylor's character grows sicker and they find no redress via newspapers, lawyers, and government agencies, the two oldtimers grow militant. In their final, grand act together, they enter the office of the mill's president, hold a gun to his head, and make him drink a Mason jar of rancid downstream water.

Jack and Taylor showed Sharyn the grave—or graves, rather—of Charlie Silver. Charlie was murdered in 1832. Parts of his body, chopped up with an ax, were discovered at different times in different locations, and he was thus laid to rest in three graves. Convicted of the crime, his young wife, Frankie, was the first woman ever executed in North Carolina, though her guilt or innocence is debated even today. It is one of the state's classic murder cases. It was Jack Pyle who, one rainy day in the late 1990s, held an umbrella over a photographer as he snapped the shot of the three graves that adorns the cover of *The Ballad of Frankie Silver*.

Jack provides me Sharyn's home address. In my letter, I describe the book I'm planning to write and ask if I can interview her. It is mid-December, which is bad timing on my part, but I understand she's at work on a new novel, and I'd love for her to tell me about it.

On December 24, I receive a Christmas card with a handwritten note: "Thanks for asking! I'll be glad to do the interview. I wish there *were* a book in progress. There is a deadline, yes, so far no book. Can it wait 'til May?"

Though it contains only a promise, the card is one of the nicest gifts I receive. Of course the interview can wait until May. That will give me time to prepare.

I write on May 4 to remind her of our tentative plan.

A reply comes ten days later. The date at the top of the page overlays part of the letterhead, and the several paragraphs of text are angled about twenty degrees off the vertical. "Blasted printer!" Sharyn has hand-scrawled across the top of the letter. She pokes fun at her state of disorganization, saying she can't find my recent letter and so is using the December one; she later signs off with "Yours in the usual chaos, Sharyn the Unready." In between, she proposes that we meet at the Reynolds Homestead—the childhood

45

home of tobacco magnate R. J. Reynolds, located in far southern Virginia—where she will be giving a program one week hence. She says we can talk for however long I like after her duty is done.

Maybe Sharyn's informality puts me too much at ease. Maybe I'm too comfortable in having read seven or eight of her novels. Or maybe I just have no idea what goes into organizing an interview. Whatever the reason, I possess an unwarranted confidence the day I drive north to Virginia.

The first sign that I'm out of my depth comes during the program. If Sharyn is disorganized, it's only in matters nonessential. Here, today, she's well coiffed, meticulously prepared, and much at ease before a gathering of fifty or sixty, most of whom seem to know her personally. Sharing the billing with her is Appalachian folk musician Betty Smith. They alternate. Sharyn reads excerpts from her Ballad novels, after which Betty performs the songs that inspired the prose. Betty has won a history-book award for a biography she's written; she has also garnered numerous music awards and has done some recordings for the Smithsonian. I've never heard of her, of course. She performs on guitar and dulcimer, which I recognize, autoharp, which sounds vaguely familiar, and something called psaltery. Music, Sharyn explains, is of such importance to her that she compiles a special soundtrack for each new novel, which she plays as she writes. I've noticed the song snippets in her books but mostly skipped over them. I resolve to purchase a Betty Smith tape after the program and to get on the ball. If I've missed the importance of music in Sharyn's books, what business do I have troubling her for an interview? They're called "the Ballad novels," for God's sake! I sulk through the rest of the program.

Afterward, Sharyn invites me to lunch with several of her friends from the audience. Then we go alone to the public library in nearby Stuart, Virginia, to talk. We find a quiet table in the back, where I set up my tape recorder between us.

"Where are you from in the mountains, exactly?" I ask.

She's not from the mountains at all, though her father was.

How could I not know that?

I grow flustered, as is reflected in my subsequent questions. They're so convoluted that they're barely recognizable as questions at all. I ramble on and on, venting literary opinions, drawing parallels where none exist, speaking on Appalachian topics with the false authority that only a native New Yorker can muster. All the while, a private voice nags me: *She's the one who's supposed to do the talking.* The tape I am making will be painful to hear. I know that much already.

Sharyn, God bless her, waits patiently until I'm finished, seeming not to judge. Her books have been translated into many languages. She's been interviewed far and wide. She's run into all manner of idiots. Her technique is to take the mess I've dumped in her lap, locate within it the germ of a pertinent question, restate that question clearly, and then answer it. I'm more thankful than I can say.

"The first time I ever lived in the mountains was in 1980. I mean, my ancestors got to Mitchell County in 1790, but between them and me came World War II. So when my father was drafted and taken out of the mountains, he ended up marrying a girl from the coast, and he never got back."

Like Sharyn's life itself, her books are neatly divided between the two distinct cultures of the lowland South and the highland South.

The heroine of her early books is forensic anthropologist and amateur sleuth Elizabeth MacPherson.

"That's my mother's side of the family," she says. "That's the flatland South. Those books are Jane Austen with an attitude. They're cultural satires."

Elizabeth MacPherson is not closely in touch with her Scottish roots. On the occasions when mountain culture does come into play—as in *Highland Laddie Gone*, which is set during a Scottish festival in the Appalachians—it is lampooned for its excesses.

Those early novels and a couple of science-fiction satires—one of them the Edgar-winning *Bimbos of the Death Sun*—were produced under trying circumstances.

"The first seven or so books were written by someone who had infant children, a day job, and was going to graduate school. Now, how much could you get done with those three things on your plate?"

"About what I'm getting done now," I admit.

"I mean literally in diapers. I mean they were infants. With *Bimbos*, for example, I was working eight to five at the Virginia Tech film library, taking two classes per semester, and I was pregnant, at the throwing-up stage, and I had a book contract that said I had to get this book written in eleven weeks. And so I would finish this job at five o'clock, get something to eat, go sit at the typewriter, and write until eleven, and then go to sleep. And cry—sometimes just cry—because I was so tired. And then get up at seven o'clock in the morning and do it again. And so I have no sympathy for people—especially twittery old ladies—who say, 'Someday, when I have the time, I'm going to write a book.' "

Those early books were successful—perhaps too much so.

"I grew up very much in this whole tradition of 'I want to be a writer,' without having any models. Nobody sits down and really talks to you about how the world works in a literary sense. So, for example, there are three ways to be known as a literary writer. You can go live in New York and work in publishing. You can get an MFA, preferably from Hollins or Iowa, or an undergraduate degree from Bennington. Or you can be a college professor, in English, at some accredited four-year school. And if you don't do one of those three things, hello genre fiction. You write *Moby Dick*, they call it 'The Hunt for White October.'

"So all of a sudden, I found myself getting typecast for writing genre fiction and getting readers with their brains in neutral, when what I wanted to do was to be taken seriously as a writer. And New York wasn't going to help me, because they were happy. As long as they can sell, you know, twenty thousand books, fifty thousand books, a hundred thousand books, they don't care if they're read by chimps. I was making money for them. 'Don't mess with anything.' But I said, 'This isn't what I want to be.'

"So what I had to do was invent my audience. About four years ago, I stopped accepting any invitations where it was, like, a mystery conference or a mystery anything. Or anybody that called me a mystery writer in publishing circles—just, no. 'You want me to come, here's what you call me, and here's what I'll talk about.' "

What you call her is an author of plot-driven literary novels, and what she likes to talk about best is her Ballad books, born of her highland heritage.

"My mother's side of the family would have been all for what Southerners consider literary writing, which is what I call 'tenure fiction,' mostly. My father's side of the family were the ones who were very strong on plot-oriented narrative. I mean, look at country songs. They're short stories. That whole Celtic tradition of using story to impart values."

"Did you have a storyteller in the family?" I ask.

"I guess my father was. I got bedtime stories. One I remember when I was three started, 'Once there was a prince named Paris whose father, Priam, was the king of Troy.' And so I got *The Iliad* in installments, but on a storytelling level, the way you might get Little Red Riding Hood."

Sharyn traces her American roots to Malcolm McCourry, a Scot who was kidnapped in 1750 and made to serve as a cabin boy on a sailing ship. After becoming an attorney in New Jersey and serving in the Revolutionary War, he arrived in the North Carolina mountains in the last decade of the eighteenth century.

Sharyn likes to describe the Appalachians as a "vertical culture." She tells how there is a vein of green-colored mineral called serpentine that runs from northern Georgia through Tennessee, the Carolinas, and Virginia and all the way up the eastern mountains to Nova Scotia, then resumes across the Atlantic in western Ireland, from which point it travels through Wales and Scotland and onward all the way to the Arctic Circle.

So it was that Malcolm McCourry and thousands of his

countrymen, vaguely dissatisfied with lowland America, gravitated to the Appalachians. They didn't know it, but the mountains were the same ones they'd lived in back home.

Sharyn says, "The most famous Appalachian writer published a book in which this sentence appears: 'There are three things we say when we want to praise our neighbors. We say, one, "I never had to shoot one of their dogs." Number two, "They keep themselves to themselves." And number three, "They don't take charity." ' Now, who was that writer?"

"Got me," I say.

"Stephen King, *Bag of Bones*. See, western Maine is the mountains, and that sentence sounds like I was describing the culture in Tennessee, Kentucky, western North Carolina. In some ways, we have more in common with the people of Maine than we do with the people of eastern North Carolina.

"I used to have a sign that said, 'Stephen King works harder than you do.' He's another one who's trying really hard to get taken seriously.

"So many people talk about literature, and they use the phrase *got through*. 'I got through X book.' As if it were a low-carbohydrate diet. As if it were the thirty-mile triathlon. Something that you endured and gritted your teeth. And people think that literature has to be like medicine. It has to be brown and taste bad. That if something is not tedious and boring, you haven't read anything of significance.

"So I thought, 'Okay, you have to be interesting, you have to have something to say. But why can't you combine it? Frost combined it. Dickens combined it. It's been done. Just because it's not fashionable doesn't mean it's not feasible.' So I just completely ignored everything after 1940 and looked back to the old novels.

"I thought, 'Why can't I be Dickens?' I wanted to be a nineteenth-century writer. I sort of realized that I missed it chronologically. But those writers—Dickens and Twain and George Eliot—were not college professors who wrote the odd book and had to edit the quarterly review. With *Oliver Twist*, Charles Dickens changed the child-labor laws. All these people had written nonfiction pamphlets and sermons, and people didn't listen because it was so depressing. And he wrote a novel and changed the child-labor laws.

"I think that somebody needs to be an advocate for the culture. I think there's been so much garbage written and especially filmed about Appalachia. And when I wrote *The Hangman's Beautiful Daughter*, there must have been a roomful of books and EPA studies on the Pigeon River. And I wrote *The Hangman's Beautiful Daughter*, in which that old man was dying of cancer because of the river, and I got letters from all over the country from people wanting to know what they should say to their congressmen. They were going to clean up that river because of an old man who didn't exist."

"Dear Fred," my letter opens, "I am writing to ask if I may interview you for a book I hope to begin soon."

For me, Fred Chappell sets the standard for long-suffering writers.

Duke University, his alma mater, is the repository of Fred's collected papers, which to date occupy eighty-four linear feet of shelf space. And that's only the part that's been cataloged. The finder's aid that describes what's in the various boxes runs sixty single-spaced pages. The collection includes drafts of his manuscripts, proofs of his books, and published material sent to him by his former students. But a large part of it—twenty boxes—is correspondence from authors famous and obscure and from an assortment of wannabes, favor curriers, and yahoos who would have Fred comment on their stories, speak to their groups, help them trace their ancestry, compose a poem for their benefit event, lend his name to their masthead, donate his time, or write them a recommendation. Fred answers every piece of mail—many thousands over the years. And they aren't perfunctory responses. If you look at Fred's notebooks—included among the papers at Duke—you'll see handwritten drafts of multipage letters to writers no one has ever heard of. And as his fame grows and word spreads that he's a soft touch, the burden only grows heavier.

I took a couple of fiction-writing workshops from Fred in graduate school. He would read all student work aloud himself in his country monotone, leaving us to guess at its authorship. After each story, he'd ask the students one by one for their comments, the odd result being that you'd have to anonymously pass judgment on your own work in front of your peers. It was either that or reveal yourself as the writer, which no one ever did.

I was never the kind of student to brown-nose or get close to my professors, Fred included. Though I was completely out of contact after graduation, he somehow knew when I took work as an editor. A couple of times a year, a manuscript would arrive from someone who'd learned about me through Fred. His memory of me was vague. I could easily recognize the parcels that came via his recommendation because they were always addressed to Steve Neal, who was the United States congressman from Fred's district at that time. But at least he remembered me—sort of.

When my first book came out, I sent a copy to him. Not then knowing his habit of answering all his mail, I had no expectation my gift would even be acknowledged. But like many others before me, I received a prompt, two-page letter complimenting the book's good points and going gently on the bad. He even quoted a couple of passages back to me. He'd read the whole thing, and closely. It remains the most gracious letter of its kind I've ever gotten.

So when I'm laying plans for my present project, it is Fred's misfortune to have been raised in the town of Canton, just west of Asheville. I will prevail on him again.

"If I understand correctly," I write, "you're planning or working on a fourth Kirkman novel. I'd like to touch base with you a few times as the book develops to find out how you're progressing. I won't ask to quote from your work or do anything other than describe it in broad terms."

Fred is enigmatic.

He's a mountain farm boy—"I sound like Gomer Pyle on a bad day," he admits—with a fancy education. He started out writing science fiction as a teenager and still has a cult following in fantasy and Gothic circles for an early novel, *Dagon*. Most highly regarded for his poetry, he is the winner of the Bollingen Prize from Yale University, the next best thing to a Pulitzer. He also claims a T. S. Eliot Award, a Rockefeller Grant, a World Fantasy Award, and a Best Foreign Novel Prize from the French Academy; like Jerry Lewis, he is said to be big in France. Noted Duke professor William Blackburn—who counted Reynolds Price, William Styron, and Anne Tyler among his students—was once cajoled into naming the best writer he'd ever taught. He didn't hesitate: it was Fred Chappell. "Anybody who knows anything about Southern writing knows that Fred Chappell is our resident genius, our shining light, the one truly great writer we have among us," novelist Lee Smith once said.

But he is also a restless soul who got kicked out of Duke for a time and took seven years to complete his undergraduate degree. The offense was "Joe College stuff," he says. "Got drunk and sassed a cop, got throwed in jail." Following that, he admits, "I was a teenager until I was forty or forty-five." Fred's detractors will always regard him as a drunk no matter how high he rises.

If his personality is complex, his body of work is downright inscrutable.

Fred's "Broken Blossoms" is as perfect a coming-of-age tale as I've ever read. In it, an eleven-year-old mountain farm boy—an easily recognizable Fred—clings to a dreamlike existence from which his father cannot shake him. His fame, the boy believes, will come as a stamp collector, or from his chemistry experiments, or from his epic science-fiction poem, "The Cycle of Varn." It's easy to envision the preadolescent Fred, like the boy, setting out from home to bring his father a jar of water where he works in the field, then arriving without the water and having no idea what happened to it, and his father taking him back home on the family wagon, its wheels cutting a straight, sensible line through the boy's footprints meandering all over the road. I can't keep a smile off my face every time I read "Broken Blossoms"; each page tops the last.

I Am One of You Forever—the first of Fred's Kirkman novels—is among my favorite books. His novel cycle was born of a poem he wrote way back in 1971. Called "The River Awakening in the Sea," it summarized Fred's feelings upon waking in bed on his thirty-fifth birthday, the same conceit that begins Dante's journey in *The Divine Comedy*.

Writing that piece got him thinking about a volume of poems sharing the theme of water. Halfway through that effort, he resolved to write companion volumes taking the other three classical elements—fire, air, and earth—as themes. Together, the volumes *River, Bloodfire, Wind Mountain*, and *Earthsleep* comprise a tetralogy called *Midquest*, recognized as Fred's major poetic work, for which he won the Bollingen. Each volume is dominated by a different part of the speaker's mountain family—*River* by his grandparents, for example, and *Bloodfire* by his father. Each covers the same twenty-four hours of the speaker's birthday at midlife, though some poems are reminiscences of the same hour in earlier years. The overall structure is complex. Each volume contains eleven poems. The first poem reflects the eleventh, the second reflects the tenth, the third reflects the ninth, and so on inward to the central sixth poem. And the forms are diverse. "Free verse and blank verse predominate," by Fred's reckoning, "but we also have terza rima, Yeatsian tetrameter, rhymed couplets, syllabics, classical hexameter variation, elegiacs, chant royal, and so forth."

Then he decided to match *Midquest* with a quartet of

novels of like setting, characters, themes, and structure. The central figure is Jess Kirkman, a boy on a mountain farm through most of the cycle. The novels have their moments—like the fine piece "The Maker of One Coffin" in *I Am One of You Forever*—but I can't help seeing Fred as a victim of his own subtlety. The novels are complex mainly for complexity's sake. A storyteller of great gifts, Fred elects instead to play puzzle maker, and the narrative suffers at times. The whole thing seems overintellectualized; its intricate structure is perceptible only to those who've had it explained to them; indeed, most garden-variety readers don't understand the Kirkman books as novels at all, but rather as story collections. Fred's indifference to popularity is always tallied on the credit side of his ledger, but I'm not sure it should be.

So it is with great admiration and a little doubt that I approach Fred at the culmination of his twenty-six years of work since "The River Awakening in the Sea," as he writes the final installment of an integrated cycle of four poetry volumes and four novels that is likely unique in all of literature.

"I can't imagine needing more than a couple hours of your time altogether—probably less—arranged however is least bothersome to you," I write. "Though it would suit me ideally if you are in fact busy on a final Kirkman book, another of your projects might prove just as interesting."

I despise my ass-kissing tone. I'm no better than the hundreds of others who will write Fred this year and ask him to get them a job or recommend them to a publisher, their own talent being insufficient for the task.

"I think my idea is a pretty good one, and I hope you'll see some merit in it."

If I were Fred, I'd tell me to go to hell, or at least neglect to answer my letter. But there's a good reason he's a beloved author and I'm not.

"Your project is an interesting one, indeed," he writes back. "And it just so happens that I have been thinking about Asheville in the very terms you broach."

Fred doesn't like to be interviewed about works in progress, but he'll be glad to talk to me about the new book once he's finished it. What he proposes for the time being is that I write him every couple of weeks. He says he'll do his best to respond with general updates on how he's coming along.

I can live with that.

Chapter 4

Toil

It isn't long before my writers' group friends begin submitting to the company where I work. They approach me shyly, apologetically. "I'm putting something in the mail to you this week" is the way a couple of them introduce it. I'm pleased at the chance to see something of theirs on paper, and say so, but I also make it clear that we're primarily a nonfiction publisher, and that most of our novel slots are filled by authors we've handled previously or who come to us with a basket of credentials.

The first to arrive is a story about two damaged men—one alcoholic and the other schizophrenic—who meet in a halfway house. After they have a falling out, the latter is tricked into being bused out of state in a scheme to keep him from receiving local government funds. The alcoholic, understanding that his estranged friend is without his medication and headed for a breakdown, tracks him down halfway across the country and brings him home. From the cover letter, I learn this about the author, one of the writers' group's stalwarts: her first husband died of chronic alcoholism, and she has both a son and a stepson who are schizophrenic.

Next is a mystery novel set in a fictional town near Asheville, in which a grizzled police chief and his pretty neophyte deputy have to solve a crime spree.

Third comes an action-packed story about a church burning in rural Georgia. Among the principals are a wealthy landowner sympathetic to the local blacks, an ex-footballing, psychologically fragile black minister, a tribe of ornery Klansmen, and a soft-spoken, do-gooding former president Jimmy Carter himself.

I write the author of the novel about the alcoholic and the schizophrenic that her approach is too didactic, that it seems she is more intent on driving home a point than spinning a good tale. And the machinations by which the schizophrenic is shipped out of state—a matter of some importance in the story—are murky.

The second submission, the genre mystery, is simply not the kind of material we publish. But since I know the author and understand that criticism will be appreciated, I take him to task for overemphasizing the young deputy's frailty and other minor matters.

I fail to flag the church-burning novel on its way in, and it is rejected by someone else on the staff before I know it has arrived.

Easily the best of the submissions is a story set mainly on a mountain farm near Asheville. A man accused of brutalizing and murdering a teenage girl is the beneficiary of a hung jury. Though it is widely agreed that he committed the crime, no witnesses were present, and there is negligible hard evidence against him. The novel then proceeds in eight alternating viewpoints as various characters—among them the older sister of the victim, her three brothers, and one of the brother's friends—try to steel themselves to extract some mountain justice. The murderer finally turns up dead, in the same remote cabin where his victim was discovered. It is the work of Sharyn McCrumb's friend Jack Pyle, who calls it "The Sound of Distant Thunder."

I'd characterize it as a literary murder novel governed by old-fashioned restraint and class. Jack does several things well. The eight narrators' voices are distinct. The humiliation of the dead girl's older sister is palpable when she has to provide details of her sex life during the courtroom scene; the devotion of her shy, long-ignored suitor could have been corny but is instead rather touching. The villain is characterized mainly by others' feelings toward him; he is physically present only on a few occasions, and then briefly; altogether, he is wisely used.

"The Sound of Distant Thunder" receives a wider circulation than my other friends' submissions. Everyone agrees to its competence, but it is ultimately rejected on the feeling that we'll likely receive several better novel manuscripts over the course of the year, an assessment I judge to be fair. I deliver the bad news by letter.

The chance of an unsolicited novel manuscript finding its way into print through a commercial publisher is remote. Where I work, the success rate is perhaps one in a thousand.

Prospects may be better at houses more noted for their fiction, but I doubt it; most of them probably don't even look at unagented material. Since the competition is so fierce, one might expect published fiction to be of consistently high quality. But in seeing the mediocre stuff on bookstore shelves, would-be novelists are understandably bewildered. They're also encouraged, believing their manuscripts are as good as most of what's out there.

When these writers submit material, they're often treated shabbily. Manuscripts are discarded unopened. Or they're opened and put directly into their return envelopes. Or they sit in a pile unexamined for six months, after which they receive a form-letter rejection. Or they find a use as scrap paper or worse. I have a good friend who once got a rejection typed on the back of page 142 of someone else's manuscript; at least it was a personal reply, he figured. In the publisher's view, material is so plentiful and available slots are so few that it doesn't make business sense to pay someone to read more than a page or two into most manuscripts, when they're read at all. Writers are so debased by the process that they're grateful for any human contact at all, even when it's a barely polite kiss-off.

Just as I expect, I receive a thank-you note from each of the three friends whose novels I turn down.

The slush pile was once a responsibility of mine. Manuscripts came in plain envelopes, in brown paper tied with string, in boxes weighing six or eight pounds, in boxes within boxes within boxes. They came registered mail, or postage due, or marked "Urgent: Unsolicited Material." Some came shoddily packed and split open, others so securely shrink-wrapped, stapled, and double duct-taped that getting into them practically required power tools. Some were already copyrighted, others elegantly laid out, still others handwritten. Some were pristine, even perfumed. Others were dog-eared or stank of cigar smoke or had what appeared to be dried snot on the pages.

They were sent by grandmothers, doctors, gradeschoolers, bereaved parents, pilots, professors, war veterans, philosophers, librarians, Libertarians, perverts, and time travelers. A surprising number came from convicts; these were written longhand and never had any return postage. The ones from foreign writers were accompanied by something called an International Postal Coupon, bearing seals peculiar to the country of origin. Since neither I nor our local post office ever figured out how these were to be redeemed in American currency, I returned foreign parcels at company expense, or didn't return them at all.

Some writers insisted on making appointments and delivering their manuscripts in person, over my protests that there wasn't a thing in the world I'd be able to tell them until I had a chance to review their material. That argument carried no weight; they showed up anyway. A few, having traveled a good distance, expected me to read their manuscripts while they sat across the desk. I once spent a surreal hour with a man who claimed to be a Gypsy and his toddler son clad in nothing but a pink diaper. Freely admitting he could neither read nor write, the man wanted me—*expected* me—to scribe his Gypsy story for him.

They sent memoirs, novels, folk tales, kids' books (though all the writers' guides clearly state that we don't publish children's material), religious tracts (though we don't handle these either), poetry (likewise), three-hundred-thousand-word whoppers, collections of newspaper columns, single short stories (though we publish only books), and antigovernment diatribes. They submitted samples beginning with page 215. They sent synopses that ran twenty-five single-spaced pages. They compared their work with *The Adventures of Huckleberry Finn, The Catcher in the Rye*, and *The Bridges of Madison County*. They judged their writing of a kind with, and even superior to, that of Jane Austen, Cormac McCarthy, and John Grisham. They hung their hats on having studied for a semester with Anne Tyler or Annie Dillard or Gordon Lish. They said how well their work would translate to the big screen, and sometimes even cast the lead roles. They claimed all their friends had read their manuscript and recommended they get it published.

"Tina was thirty-six, chronologically and in two measurements."

"They watched in horror as a slow-motion hand shut the door and oil-stained trousers and a rumpled shirt moved toward them under a scraggly mustache."

"Maybe her myopia caused her dearth of vision, her inability to see."

"Fresh from the oven, Aunt Mona brought a heaping tray of blueberry muffins, cathead-size."

"The People of the Appalachians had one thing in common: They lived in the Mountains."

"If you like my writing style but have no need of the present manuscript, I have seven others completed and ready for examination at your request, synopses below."

"My work defies a two-page outline. This is destined for a bestseller and you'll be sorry if you don't read the whole novel, guaranteed."

The competent arrived a couple of times a week, the well conceived monthly or so, the inspired once or twice a year. The great majority of manuscripts required little more than a glance to determine they were of no use to us. My assigned task was to package them and ship them back. Moved by pity, however, I often sent personal letters. What I generally got for my trouble were requests for clarification or, more likely, swiftly delivered packages containing second manuscripts that had been lying in wait, for which I'd feel obliged to send further personal correspondence. I commonly read sixty to a hundred pages when a couple of paragraphs would have sufficed. I carried manuscripts home on the weekends; my reading of published books was nil; my companions instead were "Murder on Mountain Trout Creek," "NASCAR Days and Nights," and "Bobbing Red Tulips." Two stacks of unread manuscripts on my shelves at the office grew to four, six, nine. Writers not part of my expanding circle of pen pals might wait six or seven months for a response.

They kept rattling the gates. They wore me down. I wasn't their benefactor, I came to understand. I was a naive boy.

Meanwhile, my editing—which was mainly what I was employed to do—suffered. Without reprimand—with a touch of mercy, even—the slush pile was taken from me. My company reading was thereafter limited to manuscripts that had already been through some of our readers and stood a chance of publication.

That's how I first hear of Charles Price. People around

the office start talking about a story in which a woman dies horribly of lockjaw, about a fair-haired, pale-eyed bushwhacker who calls himself Nahum Bellamy the Pilot, about a pair of grimy women riding double on a mule who come to burials to heckle the grieving, about a former slave once called Black Gamaliel. The novel has come to us in the kind of permanent binder made by copy stores, so the pages can't be divided up and circulated. All of a sudden, our company reading isn't such a burden. Rather, we're negotiating over who can have the manuscript, and for how long, and who will get it next.

Often, what appears to be support for a manuscript lasts only until the first loud contrary opinion comes along. That isn't a danger here.

Price calls his story "Held in Equal Honor," after a line from *The Iliad*. He lives near Burnsville, in the high mountains north of Asheville, but his novel is set farther west in North Carolina, in the valley of the Hiwassee River. It is the Reconstruction-era story of the Curtis family, former pillars of society brought to a lower station after the Civil War. Nahum Bellamy, the villain, wants vengeance for a wartime act to which one of the Curtis boys was party. Judge Madison Curtis, the patriarch, is incapacitated with guilt over having sacrificed a neighbor family to save his own during the war. His sons are either dead or are pale shadows of their father. It falls to Daniel McFee, the former Black Gamaliel who now rejects his old slave name, to struggle against his bitterness, discover his better nature, and come to the aid of the family that once held him in bondage.

It is actually a continuation of Price's first novel, *Hiwassee*, published by a small house and not widely traveled, though it won high praise from review sources like

USA Today, Publishers Weekly, and *Kirkus,* the toughest nut in the business. Why the new novel isn't being done by the same publisher doesn't much matter to us. We feel that what we have in our hands is superior in every regard to *Hiwassee,* which we have by now procured and passed around the office along with "Held in Equal Honor."

The best thing about working in publishing is that, every day when the postman arrives, there's a possibility that you're about to become part of something exciting, significant, and unexpected.

All of a sudden, we aren't a dumping ground for bad prose but rather players in an industry of ideas. We feel we have a winner.

My parents still embody for me many of the virtues: honesty, industriousness, thrift, foresight, perseverance, devotion, selflessness.

They did not, however, feed the family in particularly high style.

When I was in junior high, my mother worked nights and my father was responsible for supper. He had no kitchen skills and was understandably tired from his labor in a machine shop. Our definitive meals from those years were two: a large tinfoil pan of frozen Salisbury steak patties in brown gravy, which we ate twice a week, and a like-sized tinfoil pan of frozen, breaded veal cutlets in a red sauce, which we had weekly. We had no illusions about these entrées, knowing them collectively by the name of "frozen garbage." Both were served over cottage cheese—large curd—for reasons that made sense then but are mystifying to me now. We customarily had cling peaches on the side, always in heavy syrup, or canned fruit cocktail. Though a thriving garden grew in the backyard, vegetables were unaccountably absent from our table. When I went away to college, most students complained bitterly about the cafeteria fare, but it was to me a revelation. Canned ravioli, tamales in a jar, frozen pizza, little wienies in barbecue sauce, macaroni and cheese from a box, corned beef in a tin, hot dogs wrapped in bread, cheddar cheese soup or canned chicken à la king on toast—those were the foods that brought me to what maturity I attained and that I still crave today.

All of this is to say that I am not uniquely qualified for every editorial assignment that comes my way. Before beginning work on Charles Price's novel, I must finish editing the project on my desk, which happens to be a cookbook. This means a month of chervil and chipotle, of fretting over whether quantities of butter ought to be expressed in pounds, ounces, sticks, cups, or tablespoons, of wrestling long distance with an author I've never met over the fine points of Lemon Chicken Orzo Soup, Baked Brie, and Grilled Herb-Crusted Lamb Rack with Cilantro Pesto and Smoked Tomato Salsa.

So it is with much of what I edit—boating guides, travel books, folklore collections, Civil War biographies. The main requirement of the job is not expertise in a certain subject, or a literary sensibility, or even a command of the language. Rather, it's a tolerance for boredom.

But Price's novel is in line with my taste. Moreover, it doesn't call for substantial reorganization or rewriting by the editor, a blessed relief. Its problems are few and easily identifiable. First, everyone on the staff has trouble remembering the title. And the sequence of the opening chapters needs to be rearranged. And there is one flat, transparently literary scene late in the story that exists only to provide Bellamy, the antihero, a platform for examining his thoughts. Otherwise, all the novel needs is tightening.

Since I have such an easy project in hand, I enjoy a rare opportunity to do what I suppose is routine for top-drawer editors: I'll get to know the author.

I learn a few facts about Charles Price. He has just turned sixty. He is a former journalist, urban planner, and Washington lobbyist. What I don't expect is his physical appearance, when he comes down from the mountains to take lunch with some of the staff. He wears a Western jacket with a three-inch fringe, tooled leather boots that come to a long point at the toe, and a big cowboy hat. Together, they make him appear bigger than he really is. He has a ponytail, a mustache, and a triangular thatch under his lower lip. Having resigned from his stuffed-shirt career, he apparently doesn't intend going back. He draws looks from people as we walk to our restaurant table.

Charles has tended toward the writing life since childhood, when he drew comic books and sold them to his classmates. Inspired mainly by his mother, who read historical fiction, he spent his adolescence imagining himself an average person living in various periods in the past. In college, he started cultivating the persona of a writer, though he had neither skills nor credentials. He read "all the writers I thought I was supposed to, then decided I was good enough to be in their company," he says. "I was an insufferable little bastard."

In the mid-1960s, while working as a newspaperman, he wrote a novel of the Crimean War. His early, unsuccessful submissions were a Wyatt Earp novel and other Western fare—"not genre Westerns," he hastens to point out.

His devotion to writing became a point of contention in what was an unhappy marriage. Following a divorce—and much influenced in his mood by it—he wrote a medieval novel packed with murder, rape, torture, and other mayhem. One editor to whom he sent it scolded him for writing one of the most offensive things she'd ever read and then, in the same letter, invited him to submit something else. That should have told him he had talent.

In the early 1990s, Charles began making frequent trips from Washington to his native North Carolina mountains, which rekindled his love for the region and led him to see it as a canvas for his fiction. He began writing the manuscript that became *Hiwassee*.

Meanwhile, his professional career followed a downward course. He was demoted to clerical work at his lobbying firm, though he had eighteen years of service and was the senior member of the staff. A man "wedded to security," he stepped out of character and resigned one day.

A surprise was waiting in the mailbox when he got home that very evening: a book contract for *Hiwassee*, sent by the same publisher whose editor was so offended by his medieval story. It was a lightning strike. To that date, his best-known writing had been for a journal called *Airport Noise Report*.

He took his sudden success as an omen. His wasted years of spare-time scribbling were reinterpreted as "fuel," as an apprenticeship for the writing he meant to do now. He packed up and headed home. When his house in Arlington, Virginia, didn't quickly sell, a friend loaned him money for a place in Burnsville.

Hiwassee was a critical—if not a commercial—success. Charles had higher hopes for "Held in Equal Honor," but when he sent it to his publisher, it was rejected without explanation. He worked up the nerve to demand some criticism of the manuscript and subsequently got more than he reckoned. Daniel McFee, the editor wrote, was a white man in a black skin, and the novel's other black character tended so far toward the other extreme—toward defiance and belligerence—as to be cartoonish. The novel was flawed at a conceptual level. Readers would be offended by his handling of racial issues.

"Here I was, a classic Southerner trying to heal the divide," Charles says, "only to reveal myself a bigot."

"No, no," one of us protests.

"We don't see it like that at all."

"They're just afraid to touch anything racial."

Still feeling the glow of discovering something we judge special, we resolve to prove our vision of the novel the true one.

A better opportunity to get acquainted comes when Charles sends me a brochure for a writing seminar he is conducting at his house. "A day of retreat and creative expression awaits you in the beautiful Black Mountains," it promises.

"Getting Out of Your Own Way: Finding a Voice," he calls the seminar. Charles feels he has some insight to offer into how a writer can step back and let his narrative voice flow unimpeded. As for the credentials that give him authority in such matters, he summarizes the plaudits for *Hiwassee* and briefly touches on his forthcoming novel, which, knowing the old title has been rejected, he is temporarily calling "Heaven's Fire." He has circled that title on my copy of the brochure and penciled "Who knows?" in the margin.

Not having the social sense to realize that the invitation is intended as a courtesy, I promptly send in my registration fee. Better yet, I resolve to bring the whole family to the mountains.

Charles's letter acknowledging receipt of my check conveys a mild surprise. "Clearly I will have to do some heavy lifting," he predicts. With the letter comes a modest assignment: attendees of the seminar are to write an original, two-page voice piece, to be read to the entire group. Pressed for time, I consider dusting off something from my stash of unpublished gems, but I finally compose a self-consciously humorous tale about a man who writes two pages of prose for a seminar, piles his family into the car, and heads for the high country, bickering with his wife and slapping at his kids in the backseat all the way. They show up at the host's house "looking like the Joads in *The Grapes of Wrath* but acting worse."

The actual trip isn't much like that. The Black Mountains—a cross range running east and west between the Blue Ridge and the Great Smokies—contain the highest peaks east of the Mississippi. I once traveled there on a fifty-degree day in January, foolishly got off the main road, and found myself climbing a sheet of pure ice on the north slope of one of the mountains. I was scared to continue upward but more frightened at the prospect of turning around and heading down. Traffic was sparse, homes where I might obtain help sparser. If I'd gotten stuck, it would have been a week before a tow truck got my car. The place, in short, is rugged. If you get in trouble, you're likely on your own. Flatlanders generally go quiet during their trip up the switchbacks, even on a bright June day like the one that brings us to Charles Price's. We're barely aware the kids are in back.

When Charles comes out to greet us before my wife and daughters depart to see the local attractions, he is older and humbler than I recall. He is a man earning a living.

I don't envy him his task. Having received one of Charles's brochures, gentlemanly Jack Pyle offered a frank assessment of a man who, with a single published novel to his credit, feels qualified to conduct a prose-writing seminar: "He's got balls." Jack didn't know any would-be writer in the mountains who *hadn't* gotten the brochure.

Charles's blanket mailing has brought him a small group of mostly elderly, mostly amateurish penmen clustered around a table set up in his living room.

The most aggressive are two men who, respectively, having moved from California and having visited fifty countries in the course of a working career, presume that they are the star attendees and that their writing merits special attention. Charles barely has to nudge them to hear their two-page voice pieces. The Californian reads part of a forty-page story about a big-city policeman whose father is killed during a mugging. Oddly, he stresses to us that the ending will have an Oedipal tone, which seems to be an important point somehow. The world traveler reads part of a story about a May-December romance set on a barge anchored off some exotic island. Neither of these pieces meets Charles's criterion of having been written especially for the seminar, but since he's collected his money, he really isn't in a position to say anything about it.

One woman reads what she calls a "Gertrude story," about a character with whom we are all presumably familiar.

Strangest is the man who reads what sounds like a promotional piece for the Yancey County Chamber of Commerce, though he isn't associated with that organization. Hard of hearing, he speaks loudly, especially after he gets a couple of courtesy laughs.

The best excerpt, of course, is by a lady who sits quietly, waits until the end, and even then has to be prodded into reading. Hers is a story of a young American woman living in Pakistan who is threatened by locals on their way home from a religious service. They fear she's a devil woman sent to tempt them. It is understatedly exotic; I want to hear what comes next.

There are others, too.

One starts something like this: "I am sitting at my table looking out my window at a pair of bluebirds stopping to visit every bluebird box in my backyard. Would you like to come along?"

Charles is obliged to be kind, but I suspect it is his nature anyway. He gets the writers to describe the larger works into which their two-page pieces fit; he deftly extracts the few bits of coal from the heaps of slag; he identifies the places where the voice could be made more personal and the writing more vivid; he sees possibilities; he sets a tone of hope.

But it isn't until after lunch and a recess that he takes center stage. During the break, he encourages us to explore what we can of the mountain and to write our impressions of it. Tired from my trip, I do the former but not the latter, walking the stream-skirting gravel track uphill from Charles's house. Those who do the writing assignment are rewarded with a second critique weighing their new pieces against the ones they brought from home. Charles focuses on what is generally the greater immediacy and the truer voice of the writing done on his mountain.

Following this, he gives us a couple of concrete examples of how to revise. One comes as a surprise: the closing of Abraham Lincoln's First Inaugural Address. Charles traces Lincoln's revisions through a couple of drafts, showing point by point how he refined the language. The second example treats the evolution of one of Charles's own scenes, in which a young boy, attracted by some swarming blue-black butterflies, finds they are hovering about—and even beginning to consume—a human corpse. It isn't drawn from either *Hiwassee* or the new novel, though I recognize the boy character. It makes me wonder what else Charles has in reserve.

Last comes a pep talk about how artistry is less a divine gift for a chosen few than it is a possibility for ordinary people who would only exercise diligence. Then and there, it seems a promise for each of us.

Altogether, my afternoon of eavesdropping on Charles's life leaves me reassured of his talent, though I regret he is getting a late start in the game and is having to sing for his supper.

CHAPTER 5

Critiquing the Critiquer

In June 1922, Thomas Wolfe headed home from his graduate studies at Harvard upon learning that his father was gravely ill. He was fifty miles from Asheville when he read in a local newspaper that W. O. Wolfe was dead.

Wolfe spent that summer at home. There's an oft-told story of how he and a friend were taking two girls for an outing on Sunset Mountain one day when the car they were driving suffered a flat tire. They were in the process of changing it when an elderly man in dungarees walked out of the forest and offered a hand. They accepted, and the job was soon accomplished. As he and his friends departed, Wolfe handed the old man a quarter, which he welcomed with a bow.

Several years afterward, Wolfe's brother Frank supposedly asked the man, Edwin Wiley Grove, the owner of the Grove Park Inn, if he returned or spent the quarter. "No, I still have it," Grove said. "First I kept it because it was the only tip I ever received, and then its preciousness grew in proportion to Tom's fame."

Grove died two and a half years before the publication of *Look Homeward, Angel*—that is, before Thomas Wolfe achieved anything approaching fame. So the question becomes whether Grove was a seer or whether the chance meeting between Asheville's great literary son and its most influential man was apocryphal.

E. W. Grove had no need of stray coins from a pauper like Thomas Wolfe. As a young pharmacist in Paris, Tennessee, in the 1870s, he had pioneered a formula for suspending quinine in a liquid and making it nearly tasteless. Malaria was a scourge in the South in those days, but many people resisted quinine because of its bitter flavor. Grove's compound, Feberlin, was sold by prescription.

His real breakthrough came when he developed an over-the-counter version of the same formula, plus sugar, lemon flavoring, and iron. He called it Grove's Tasteless Chill Tonic. Fortunately for Grove's pocketbook, quinine hindered the growth of malaria but could not actually kill it. It was therefore recommended that people take four teaspoons of Grove's elixir daily throughout the entire two-month malaria season. Even when the threat of the disease waned, the tonic was successfully marketed as a product that "restores Energy and Vitality by creating new, healthy blood" and "makes children and adults as fat as pigs." In the late 1890s, it outsold another recent Southern concoction, Coca-Cola. Grove also developed the first cold tablet, which he sold as Grove's Laxative Bromo Quinine. He was a millionaire several times over.

Like many others, Grove came to Asheville for health reasons, hoping the mountain air would provide relief that his own medicines could not from his bronchitis, chronic insomnia, and debilitating bouts of hiccups, which sometimes lasted for months. Grove's business interests broadened over the years. He founded a newspaper in Atlanta and invested in real estate in Georgia, Arkansas, Florida, and North Carolina. He bought most of Sunset Mountain on Asheville's northern boundary and began selling residential lots in a development he called E. W. Grove Park.

It was 1909 when he conceived the Grove Park Inn. Grove favored the great inns of Yellowstone Park—the Old Faithful Inn in particular—but the several architectural firms he auditioned failed to come up with an acceptable plan for a similar hotel on Sunset Mountain. It was Grove's talented son-in-law, Fred Seely, a man with no training whatsoever in the field, who finally drew the sketch that was followed almost exactly for the inn's exterior.

In July 1912, Grove's architectural engineer began hiring a crew of four hundred local men, many of whom walked away from other employment at the prospect of Grove's dollar-a-day wage. Mule teams, trucks, a single steam shovel, and hand tools were the workers' only aids. Grove boldly announced that the inn would be completed in slightly less than a year.

One of the principal tasks was the hauling of boulders, some weighing five tons, from nearby mountains for the inn's six-story walls, which were four feet thick at the base. Workers were instructed to set them in place just as they found them, moss and lichen intact. The most spectacular feature of the inn is its great hall, which has a thirty-six-foot-wide fireplace at either end, each of which was assembled from a hundred and twenty tons of granite boulders and could accommodate twelve-foot logs atop its five-hundred-pound andirons. The inn was completed by July 12, 1913, only twelve days behind schedule. Secretary of State William Jennings Bryan gave an address at the opening.

In the early days, the emphasis was on enforced tranquility and hyper-cleanliness. Guests were discouraged from bringing small children. Automobiles were barred from entering the property from ten-thirty at night until nine in the morning. Guests were asked not to run water or make unnecessary noise at night; indeed, the water flow to their rooms was cut off at ten-thirty. Those in the great hall needed to keep their voices low. Anyone who didn't was handed a printed card requesting compliance. The purity of the inn's water was checked each month. All dishes were boiled—twice, in fact—after every use. Coins exchanged at the desk were cleaned by machine at night.

In addition to the garden-variety rich, Woodrow Wilson came, as did Calvin Coolidge, Herbert Hoover, William Howard Taft, Franklin and Eleanor Roosevelt, Dwight and Mamie Eisenhower, Richard Nixon, the Mayo brothers, John D. Rockefeller, Charles Schwab, Henry Ford, Thomas Edison, Harvey Firestone, Enrico Caruso, Harry Houdini, Al Jolson, Will Rogers, Bill Tilden, Bobby Jones, Billy Graham, Norman Vincent Peale, and many others through the years. Two major wings—one nine stories, the other eleven—were added at either end of the old inn in the 1980s, bringing the total number of rooms to over five hundred.

Some guests who knew the inn in years past bemoan the din in the great hall today. But the money and the luminaries keep coming—the elder George Bush, Henry Kissinger, Anthony Hopkins, Jack Lemmon, Arnold Palmer, Michael Jordan, on and on.

Scott Fitzgerald's is the best-known author's stay, but Alex Haley, Helen Keller, Charles Frazier, George Plimpton, and others have also been guests. Margaret Mitchell honeymooned here.

Once his great hotel was completed, Grove set about remaking Asheville's downtown. He bought out and razed his main competition, the Battery Park, where George Vanderbilt had stayed before he began amassing land for the Biltmore Estate. What's more, Grove chopped off seventy-five feet of the hill on which the Battery Park Hotel stood and hauled off the dirt in trucks. In its place, he built a second Battery Park, taller but less grand and sprawling. In April 1925, Babe Ruth was brought to the new hotel after collapsing at the Asheville train station upon arriving for an exhibition game. His coach scoured the town for a pair of size forty-eight pajamas for decency's sake, since the Babe normally slept nude. The best he could find was a size forty-two—in hot pink. Ruth's difficulty was variously explained as the flu, acute indigestion, an intestinal abscess, and a case of poisoning, but he most likely had the clap. Newspapers abroad reported him dead. The incident, known in baseball circles as "the Bellyache Heard Round the World," kept him off the field for the better part of a season at the peak of his career.

Grove's crowning glory was to be the Grove Arcade, a

forerunner of today's shopping malls. It was to occupy a full city block across the street from the Battery Park Hotel. The main entrance, facing north, was guarded by a pair of griffins; grotesque heads were carved all the way around the exterior. Inside was to be an array of oak-fronted shops, mezzanines, and spiral staircases. On top, a roof garden with a band shell was planned. Rising from the center of the arcade was to be a fourteen-story office tower.

Grove laid the foundation in 1926 and died in 1927, and the central section was built to a height of only four stories. The arcade has just recently been renovated for upscale apartments and shops and opened to the public. Obviously truncated but nonetheless grand, it will likely never be completed as envisioned.

Having spent my few overnight visits to Asheville in forty-dollar motels, I jump at the chance for a room in the Grove Park Inn, courtesy of the largest writers' organization in the state.

Each fall, the eighteen-hundred-member guild sponsors a three-day conference attended by about five hundred writers. The annual event rotates among posh sites around the state.

I am to be a fourth-tier celebrity. Famous writers are brought in to give talks or readings during the weekend's luncheons and dinner banquets; they generally arrive and depart quickly and have little personal contact with the attendees. Then come modestly successful authors like my new friend Charles Price, who conduct seminars for classroom-sized groups on sundry topics like "The Scuppernong

Connection," "The Seven Deadly Sins of Science Fiction Writing," and "Finding Form, or What's a Nice Sonnet Like You Doing in a Place Like This?" Then come the agents, publishers, and marketing specialists who participate in round-table discussions. Finally come the worker bees like me, who review twenty-page manuscript samples one on one with conference attendees.

Actually, my presence at the conference is contingent on proof of my popularity. Only a small percentage of attendees will pay the fee to have their work critiqued. Those participating select their editor from a list of six, the other five of whom are from national publishers noted for their fiction. No one comes to such conferences to learn how to write nonfiction, my company's specialty, which doesn't bode well for my chances. The guild informs me that if a minimum three people don't select me, I will have no room at the inn—though, to my possible chagrin, my photograph and capsule biography will have already run in the conference brochure. I served the same function at the previous fall's conference in a different city. Sure enough, only two writers chose me, and ultimately just one of them was able to attend.

But maybe news of my diligent work is spreading and I am finally making a name for myself in the business. Word comes back that I've been chosen by six aspiring authors, the maximum number allowed—wise souls all.

I make the drive to Asheville and wind my way up Sunset Mountain to the great stone inn. I am to be housed in the Vanderbilt Wing, Room 4057, which happens to be the Cyd Charisse Room. My antennae raised to all things writerly, I note the George Will Room and the Deepak Chopra Room on my way there.

I reread my manuscript samples after settling in. It's difficult to spend a thirty-minute private session critiquing a scant twenty pages of material without schoolmarming the writer about punctuation and grammar. This will be especially true in four of my six cases, since the writers haven't provided synopses and I have no idea where their stories are headed and therefore little to talk about.

One sample is from a murder mystery whose heroine works in the insurance industry and also happens to be a champion golfer. The author has broken her opening scene into two separate chapters for no good reason I can discern.

Another is from a New York novel about two twenty-something, high-aspiring black girls who meet through their dead-end office jobs. Since one of the heroines starts a new position, makes a best friend, goes out with her boyfriend, and begins an involvement with another man all within the span of twenty pages, I'll advise the writer to slow the pace and spend more time establishing her characters and setting.

Another has just the opposite problem. A "grit lit" story of a Southern family dealing with a visiting wayward uncle, it is all personal background and no forward movement.

Another concerns the friendship between a professional woman and a mental patient. It's self-consciously literary and transparently autobiographical.

Another tells of hard times in an enclave of Norwegian immigrants. The author begins her sample with page 43, which makes it difficult to pick up on the action.

The best of the samples by far comes from a kind of

retro/techno thriller set on an air-force base in West Germany during the Cold War. The antihero, a decorated American fighter pilot, murders his underage German lover and has to dispose of the body. A conflicted man whose patriotism overlays a family history of suicide, a cigar-chomping enigma in his trademark cucumber-green sunglasses, he makes a promising villain indeed. The writer's cover letter takes pains to explain that, while he understands that his submission is not to exceed twenty pages, he has taken the liberty of including additional pages to close out a chapter.

Apology accepted. I wouldn't have stopped reading anyway.

A keynote presentation by Jan Karon, open-mike readings by conferees, "Three Uses of the Knife: How the Blues Works As a Literary Device," "Feeding the Ancient Fires: American Indians Writing Their Own Literature," "Romance Sells!"—all this takes place before my arrival.

My first obligation is a session called "Meet and Greet with Editors and Agents," in which hopeful writers are set loose en masse upon a small number of publishing professionals. The inn's countless meeting rooms notwithstanding, the event only merits space in a crowded hallway around two tables of crackers and cheese and soft drinks. It is the kind of thing people in the business approach with trepidation—an open-air market of bad ideas, shouted above a din.

I've barely pinned on my nametag before a manuscript sample is thrust at me—some kind of mountain memoir by an instructor at a community college. She says she spoke to me about it some months previously, though I have no such recollection. I tuck the sample under my arm.

Then comes a nattily dressed black couple, the man in a preacher's collar. They have a fifty-five-page complete manuscript that the woman starts reading to me unbidden; I gather it has to do with Jesus but can't understand much of what she's saying because of the noise. I suggest that they'll need more than fifty-five pages to make a book and tell them how to compile a list of publishers of religious material. The looks on their faces indicate that they've understood me about as well as I have them. I'm starting to sweat.

Rescue comes in an unlikely form. "You're Stephen Kirk," a sixtyish man with close-cut hair and glasses informs me. "I recognize you from your picture."

In his arm atop a small pile of papers is a copy of my book, an unlikely sight that pleases me deeply. The placement of his bookmark suggests he has read only about fifty pages, but someone with my track record shouldn't complain. I like this man.

He is Bryan Aleksich, the author of my Cold War thriller.

"I know we're not supposed to have our session until tomorrow morning," he says, "but I was hoping we could discuss my sample now. Do you have time?"

My stack of twenty-page manuscript excerpts is in the Cyd Charisse Room. I'd planned to make notes on the samples later in the evening. But unlike the other submissions, his story has stuck in my mind down to the characters' names, and I already know what I want to tell him. And meeting with him now will buy me a graceful exit from the "Meet and Greet" session.

Off the writer-choked hallway is an empty conference room—where the "Meet and Greet" should have been held. We adjourn there.

I soon understand that Bryan is given to frank speech.

"I've been enjoying your book. I just picked it up last night," he says. "I wish they'd designed a different cover, though. I'm sorry they used that picture."

Bryan tells me he has a degree in graphic arts. He describes how the cover would have been improved by using a pen-and-ink illustration instead of a photograph.

"I have to say I don't care for the title either," he says. "It's too familiar."

I'm not sure how to respond. I've always liked the cover, though I'm not so certain just now.

Bryan smiles thinly. "You were my third choice."

I ask what he means.

"We had to pick three people from the list to review our manuscripts, in case we couldn't get who we wanted. The editor from Algonquin was my first choice. I was also interested in the woman from St. Martin's."

I can't argue with his choices. I'd have done the same in his position, though I hope I'd keep the knowledge to myself.

I don't take Bryan to be mean-spirited. Apparently, he places a premium on up-front honesty. If so, I can provide him a dose, too. "Let's talk about your sample," I say.

Most of what I tell him is positive. I admire the way Bryan describes the suicide of the antihero's brother in a single, spare paragraph. I like the couple of details he uses to physically describe the antihero. I find the murder of the German girl downright chilling.

I can tell he's flattered.

"But I wouldn't try to sell it as an illustrated novel," I say. In fact, the title page proclaims exactly that: "An Illustrated Novel." The first page of each chapter carries a drawing of a vintage airplane. "Illustrated novels are for kids. You're giving publishers an easy reason to reject you. Sell the story first. Then, if you find some interest, you might say you've got illustrations they're welcome to look at. But don't be surprised if they say no. They've got their own illustrators."

If I anticipate some resistance to this suggestion, then I underestimate the willingness of struggling writers to seize any ray of hope. Bryan wants success uncommonly badly. He is willing to hold his illustrations in reserve or to do anything else that might help his novel see print. "I don't even need an advance," he generously offers.

Bryan, I learn, is seventy-two—a good ten years older than I guessed. The son of Serbian immigrants, he went to work in the Pittsburgh steel mills at age fifteen during World War II. He later studied graphic arts, then drew for an architectural firm in California, then went to law school at UCLA. More pertinent to his manuscript, he is also a former fighter pilot. He was accepted into pilot training at age twenty-five—just under the cutoff—having overcome an eye problem that required him to get a muscle surgically cut and having somehow passed his physical despite congenital high blood pressure.

Two days before Christmas 1965, Bryan was flying an Air National Guard nighttime training mission in the Los Angeles area. His two-seat trainer was to serve as a target for a pair of F-102 fighters. Reaching his assigned altitude of forty thousand feet required him to fly his aged jet at 100 percent power for forty-five minutes—fifteen minutes beyond its designed capacity. When he reached altitude and reduced power, the engine blew. Bryan drifted for several minutes until the plane lost enough altitude for him to eject safely. From fourteen thousand feet, he parachuted to the Mojave Desert through heavy cloud cover, fighting nausea as he dropped, unable to see the ground below him. Luckily, he landed on a ridge; a short distance to either side and he would have tumbled down a steep slope. He spotted a line of car lights in the distance that indicated a road. Bryan made himself as comfortable as he could for the evening, hiked to the road upon rising the next morning, hitched a ride to the nearest telephone, and notified the base of his whereabouts.

A couple of weeks after that, he sat down and started his novel. In the 1950s, he'd served a tour at an air base in West Germany, which would provide his setting. A heavily modified version of his fall from forty thousand feet was to be the climactic scene.

By 1970, he had a 250,000-word manuscript. He self-published a thousand copies, sold about two hundred of them, then reread the novel and found it dreadful. Bryan took an electric drill and bored a hole through each of the remaining eight hundred copies, to make it less likely they'd be picked up by strangers. Then he took them to the dump.

But he'd caught the bug. By 1988, the revamped story was down to about half its original length. Bryan inquired with an agent, who indeed wanted to handle the novel. Over the next five years, it was rejected by nearly sixty publishers.

In 1993, Bryan retired from legal practice and left California for the North Carolina mountains south of Asheville. The following year, he signed up for a basic writing course through *Writer's Digest*. He next took an advanced program offered by the magazine, then asked if he could pay for an additional six months of instruction. Bryan completed the program with increased confidence, a high level of enthusiasm, and a manuscript that was another ten thousand words leaner.

So here he was with a novel thirty-some years in the making, never having earned a dime off his writing but still attending conferences, still hoping for a greater editor when he was assigned a lesser one, still enrolling in a seminar in mystery writing here and a class in expository writing there, more clear-headed about his prospects than in years past but still stubbornly hopeful.

What I want to know is why a man who was a fighter pilot and a lawyer—either one a life's accomplishment for most people—feels such a need to be a novelist, too.

Not getting an immediate response from Bryan, I prod. Since it requires nothing, really, beyond pencil, paper, and one's own experience, is writing the cheapest way to immortality? Though no one is averse to money and recognition, don't writers want most of all to leave behind something of value?

He scoffs at this. "Then they ought to spend more time learning their craft."

We talk for a while about other things—my family, the house where he lives, the route he traveled to reach the conference.

Then comes this from Bryan: "You say you enjoyed my

sample. I have the complete manuscript in my room. Would you be willing to take it home with you?"

I've been told the food at the Grove Park Inn is mediocre but that the authors who'll be manning the microphone during meals are first-rate. On the contrary, we all enjoy a fine dinner but endure a dreadful reading that evening.

The next morning, I meet with the six writers assigned to me. The author of the golf-course murder mystery is a neatly dressed woman in her sixties. The writer of the story about the two black friends in New York is a six-foot, distractingly pretty white girl. The man who wrote of the Southern family and its wayward uncle is painfully shy and wears an earring. The lady with the novel about the professional woman and the mental patient has indeed written from experience. The woman with the story about the ethnic enclave has plans to self-publish her book and direct-market it to Norwegian-interest societies. The final writer, Bryan, brings me his complete manuscript. I talk the full half-hour with each of them.

All my responsibilities met, I tour the old part of the inn before leaving the conference. Scott Fitzgerald stayed in Room 441 and the adjoining 443. I reach the top of the fourth-floor stairs at the same moment the elevator arrives.

I must look lost.

"Can I help you with something?" the elevator operator asks.

I tell her my purpose.

"Oh, certainly. Let's see if it's empty." She leads me down the hall.

One of Fitzgerald's former rooms is occupied, but the other is being prepared for an afternoon arrival.

"Go in and take a look. Most of the furnishings in the old part of the inn are original, though I can't say for sure about his room."

The old rooms are smaller and much more spartan than the ones in the new wings. I'm not sure which of the two rooms is which, but this may be where the great writer, one hot and sleepless night a couple of weeks after breaking his shoulder, tripped and fell while making his way to the bathroom. Unable to get to his feet because of his body cast, he spent forty-five minutes—from four o'clock to nearly five—in crawling to the telephone to summon help. He subsequently developed arthritis in his shoulder and was confined to bed for several weeks. It was during that period, and perhaps in this room, that he twice attempted suicide.

The cleaning girl is embarrassed, as am I. She busies herself in a corner. I don't linger long.

Poet James Seay shares my interest in literary ghosts. He once found Faulkner's resting place with no more to go on than the memory of a couple of old oak trees he'd seen in a photo of the author's burial. He's been as far afield as Moscow, to seek out Boris Pasternak's grave.

"I have spent time in out-of-the-way rooms," Seay has written, "rooms where people whose work I care about came and left something. It's my theory that gifted people generate a tremendous energy—though it need not always be manifest on the surface—and a residuum of that energy is left behind in places, especially rooms, where the gifted burned up part of their gift."

Seay once piled a witch-medium and five of her acolytes into a station wagon and led them up the mountains to Asheville, where they held a seance in one of Fitzgerald's old rooms at the Grove Park Inn. Seay brought a couple of Fitzgerald objects with him: a brown paper bag containing a copy of the "Crack-Up" articles and a book with photos of the author, tape covering the spine so the witches couldn't identify it. They were unaware of Fitzgerald's association with the inn. Indeed, they probably knew little of the man.

After some heavy sweating and a few guttural utterances around the table, one of the acolytes took a pen and wrote down a psychic transmission coming in from the other realm. It said, simply, "Damn You Love," which Seay took as a possible manifestation of what Fitzgerald meant when he commented that "the test of a first-rate intelligence is the ability to hold two opposed ideas in the mind at the same time, and still retain the ability to function." Two names also came over the wire: Tony and Gloria. Seay supposed them to refer to Anthony and Gloria Patch of *The Beautiful and Damned*.

That's pretty slim pickings given the trouble he went to in organizing the event, but his results were still better than mine.

It is nine or ten days after the conference when I receive in the mail a photocopy of my book's cover, along with a same-sized mock-up of Bryan Aleksich's proposed redesign. Of course, I have copies of my own book and don't need a xerox of its cover. I suspect he has sent both covers so I can compare them on equal terms. I also suspect he is the kind of man who will feel indebted to me for reading his manuscript and so is trying to offer something of value in return. Still, the cover is a dead issue for me. Unsure of an appropriate response to Bryan's gift, I don't respond at all.

Four weeks later, I get a call from him asking if he can send replacement pages for a small section of his manuscript he's reworked. I confess that I've been busy with my own writing and have read only to about page 80.

"Oh, are you finding it tough going?" he asks.

I assure him not.

Bryan proposes that I drop him a note when I'm done reading, after which he'll phone me at home to discuss the manuscript at length.

His call spurs me, and I finish the novel a week later. Its promising opening notwithstanding, the manuscript has structural problems. Too much space is given the mating dance of the air base's pilots and love-lorn women. Even the flight scenes, which are Bryan's special pride—a mock dogfight, a thunderstorm sequence—need a better context so they don't become ends in themselves. It matters little that Bryan has been writing the story for well over three decades. It still needs another draft.

I call to tell him all this. I catch him unaware; he wanted to be the one to phone me. I sense that I'm low-bridging him, though my intention is only to talk while the details are still in my mind. He leaves the line briefly to turn down his music; he fumbles for a pencil or his glasses. But he recovers quickly. He listens without argument or bitterness; he queries me on aspects of the story I haven't brought up; he makes notes throughout; he takes the criticism just as it is meant; he continues to see the possibility of success.

When I return his manuscript a couple of days later, I include a cover letter I hope will soothe any hurt feelings. "You don't strike me as someone who needs to have things sugar-coated," it reads in part, "so what you got the other day over the phone was my honest opinion. What I may not have expressed very well is my admiration for what you've accomplished. I think you've brought the novel most of the way to where it needs to be."

It crosses in the mail a gracious two-page letter from Bryan thanking me for my time.

I still want to understand what writing means to him. Say he continues revising his novel until he grows infirm but never finds a publisher. How will that rank among the disappointments of his life? Is his writing an avocation or a need? Is he near the point of quitting?

I receive an indirect answer to this last question five days later, when Bryan calls me at work. He says he had written the editor at Algonquin who was his first choice to review his manuscript sample at the conference. He has sent that editor fifty dollars—the same fee he paid for my services—and his first two chapters in the hope that the editor will now provide him a conference-style evaluation like the one he and I had in Asheville.

He tells me this by way of background. The reason for his call is that, since writing the Algonquin editor, he has received his manuscript back from me and has noted the marks I made regarding grammar, punctuation, word choice, repetition, and the like. He is wondering if he ought to send the editor replacement pages.

I tell him that what he has requested of the editor is rather unusual and that, no, he shouldn't send replacement pages. All the same, I have to admire his moxie.

Sometime during our conversation, I tell Bryan about my Asheville-area writers' group and invite him to attend. I also describe the book I'm working on and confess my selfish interest in him and his novel.

CHAPTER 6

Cornucopia

Where I live, the spring rains are quickly forgotten. Unless you water heavily, the ground begins to crack around the Fourth of July, and unshaded grass crunches underfoot like dry cereal. The air is humid, and the skies most summer afternoons fill with storm clouds, but any promise of moisture goes unfulfilled nine times out of ten. By late August, it might take you an hour to dig a hole big enough to plant a sapling, if you cared to try.

But this year is an exception. The previous summer having been so parched that many towns instituted water restrictions, the unusually heavy winter rains are welcome. By early spring, the reservoirs are replenished and the rivers are running at normal levels. By mid-spring, they're topped off. But spring conditions continue halfway into summer, and flooding results. People who've had bone-dry basements for thirty years now have standing water. Mold begins to grow, starting underneath houses and working its way upward. An employee at a local hardware store tells me he's selling fifty dehumidifiers a week.

One Saturday, I brave our crawlspace to check for moisture and mold. Low and thick with cobwebs, it's one of my least favorite places. At times, I'm flat on my belly squeezing under the water pipes, pulling myself along by my fingernails almost. It takes me forty-five minutes to make the circuit. There are puddles in a few places and, yes, what I take to be mold.

Upon emerging, I'm covered with red-clay mud from top to bottom, front and back. It's the dirtiest I've been since I was a kid—maybe ever. When I step in the back door to the kitchen, I learn the girls are out of sight upstairs, so I strip to my undershorts and throw my clothes out onto the deck, to be dealt with later.

The phone rings. I'm close to it, but I ask my wife to answer, since I don't want to touch anything. I can hear that it's a woman.

My wife hands me the phone.

"This is Gail Godwin."

I'm better prepared than I was the first time I thought about approaching her. I've read several of her books and what print interviews and biographical material I've been able to find.

But you'd never take me for an ace interviewer looking at me now.

I wrote her a blind letter introducing myself, describing my book project, and asking for fifteen minutes of her time. Not knowing her preference for a means of responding, I gave her my home address, home phone, work phone, and e-mail address. I had no real expectation of hearing from her at all. If I did, I suspected it would be by mail, not by phone at home on a Saturday morning. This is not meant as a complaint by any means, but rather as a token of my surprise.

I tell her about the rain, the mold, and the crawlspace, my free hand flailing futilely in my attempt to explain why I'm unable to talk just now. I finally calm down and ask if I can call her back a couple of days hence, to which she graciously agrees.

Gail Godwin is not so much a mountain author as she is an author who happens to be from the mountains. Fred Chappell and Robert Morgan, for example, explore their themes in the context of Appalachian culture in almost all the fiction they write. But Godwin doesn't like to keep treading the same ground.

"My settings move as I move," she tells me during our subsequent conversation. "It has to do with a writer's quest, what she or he is trying to do, what theme attracts them. One of my themes that attracts me has always been how to move on, how to change the spirit—however, whatever it is—rather than staying in one place and getting to know all the levels and sublevels, like Faulkner."

But something about her protagonist Margaret Gower has kept the author herself from moving on. The 1999 novel *Evensong* interests me partly because it's the only sequel Godwin has ever written.

Margaret, the principal character in *Father Melancholy's Daughter*, is six years old when Madelyn Farley, a long-lost friend of her mother's, comes for a visit to the family's home in Virginia. Madelyn lives the kind of artistic existence Margaret's mother has given up for her stifling life as the wife of a small-town Episcopal priest who is too old for her and suffers from depression. On the afternoon following Madelyn's arrival, no one picks up Margaret at the bus stop. Her mother, it turns out, has accompanied Madelyn on her return north. At first, Margaret's father tells his congregation and his daughter that the trip will reinvigorate his wife's spirit. But months pass and she fails to return. Margaret's mother subsequently dies in a car wreck while traveling in England with Madelyn, leaving her daughter uncertain if she ever would have come home and even if she was having a lesbian affair. *Father Melancholy's Daughter* is told from Margaret's perspective as a college senior.

The tragedies in Godwin's life have been known to find their way into her fiction. Her half-brother's murder of an ex-girlfriend and his subsequent suicide were recast as central events in *A Southern Family*. Godwin's mother died in a car accident near Asheville two years before the publication of *Father Melancholy's Daughter*.

Gail Godwin was born in Alabama, her parents, both North Carolinians, having taken temporary residence there for her father's job as manager of a lakeside resort. Her parents soon divorced, after which mother and daughter came to live with Godwin's grandmother in the North Carolina mountain town of Weaverville and then on Charlotte Street in Asheville.

During World War II, the wives of servicemen had an easier time finding work than did divorcées. When people asked the whereabouts of Gail's father, Kathleen Godwin told them he was fighting the war, which was true, since he was in the navy. After the war, she said he'd died in the fight. When he finally came to Asheville to visit, she claimed he was Gail's uncle.

Kathleen Godwin did just fine without a man. In the mornings, she taught drama, poetry, or creative writing at one school and composition and Spanish at another. In the afternoons, she wrote for the Asheville newspaper. In her later years, Julia Wolfe became enamored of her son's fame and would call the paper whenever she recalled another anecdote from Tom's youth. Kathleen Godwin was the writer dispatched to cover those stories.

"That was so funny," Gail tells me. "Mother would come home and say, 'Well, Julia called again today. She remembered something else about Tom.'

"Her beat during the war years was mainly Oteen, where all the wounded servicemen were. She also covered famous visitors to town. I remember Bela Bartok spent a summer writing music there. She was sent over because the only language they had in common was French. Hers wasn't very good, but she was able to interview him in French. Oh, and when Mrs. Roosevelt would come to visit the servicemen in the hospital, Mother always got her. Mother was so impressed that Mrs. Roosevelt always remembered people's circumstances and names. She would always say, 'And how's your little girl, Gail?'

"And then whenever Mrs. Wolfe called, Mother would go over to the Old Kentucky Home with her spiral notepad."

Gail's grandmother took care of the household chores

while Kathleen "went out in all weathers to bread-win for us like a man," according to Gail. On the weekends, Kathleen earned two cents a word writing romance stories for pulp magazines. She wrote under her own name and a pseudonym, Charlotte Ashe.

Gail attended St. Genevieve-of-the-Pines Academy, a Catholic school in Asheville.

"The thing about the nuns was, we had to write so much," she tells me. "I wonder if children have to write so much today. We were always writing something. We had to do book reviews, book reports. We had to make a magazine and put stories in it, advertisements, and create the entire magazine ourselves. They were very generous about reading your stuff. I had this one nun, I would write stories in a notebook, and then she would read them on the bus home. We weren't allowed to talk; we sat silently. She would read my stories and then give me a little sign language that they were good."

But when I ask who was more important to her writing, there is no doubt.

"Let's see, as they say on the grand jury, which I'm serving on now, 'On a scale of one to ten, where's the pain?' On a scale of one to ten, I would say my mother's influence over my writing was an eight, and the nuns were a five. Of course, that adds up to more than ten."

The sway our parents' lives hold over our own is one of the issues examined in *Evensong*. Margaret Gower Bonner ostensibly leads her father's life. She is now an Episcopal priest at a church in a North Carolina mountain town patterned partly after Highlands, southwest of Asheville. But it is her mother's legacy that weighs on her. Like her mother, she has married a priest considerably older than she is. Adrian Bonner has a keen intellect like her father but none of the humor to go with it. He is emotionally arrested and sexually ambivalent, twin products of his childhood in an orphanage. He's also sickly. Temptation enters the story in the person of Madelyn Farley, the same woman who once stole Margaret's mother. Margaret has traveled with Madelyn to Europe—to her mother's death site, even. She has met Madelyn's artsy friends and felt the pull of their lifestyle. She has even cared for Madelyn in her infirmity. A critical juncture in the novel comes when Margaret is willed Madelyn's New York apartment and travels north to dispose of the property. Or will she take the apartment herself, heed the call of the broader world, and forsake her tired life with Adrian? Does she have the strength of character to be someone other than her mother's daughter?

My only chance to look at the Gail Godwin Papers at the University of North Carolina is on a Saturday, when the special-collections library closes at one. By the time I make the ninety-minute drive from my home, find a parking deck off campus, walk the half-mile to the library, and sign the forms that allow me access to the collection, it's a little past nine-thirty.

The forty-plus linear feet of materials, thousand-plus folders, and twelve-thousand-plus items encompass drafts and proofs of Gail's novels; plot, character, and theme notes; research matter; financial records; notebooks; early writings penned under various names; some of her mother's writings; photograph albums; texts of speeches; audiovisual records of some of Gail's public appearances; correspondence with publishers and editors; correspondence with authors like Kurt Vonnegut, Joyce Carol Oates, John Irving, and John Updike; teenage scrapbooks; school mementos; diaries; yearbooks; drawings; items related to her mother's death and half-brother's murder-suicide; even letters from the child witness to the crime.

I barely have time to drink a drop from the ocean.

I'm most interested in Kathleen Godwin's writings. I find some complete issues of romance magazines, as well as pulled pages containing only Kathleen's stories. "Home Is the Hero," from the October 1945 *All-Story Love*, carries the teaser, "One girl collected medals. Did the other collect hearts?" There's also "Memory of a Love Song" from *Love Short Stories* ("Cam was the man Jeanie loved—and his faithless fiancée was her best friend!"), Charlotte Ashe's "Dangerous Kisses" ("Intrigue and love went hand in hand when Pam kissed a handsome stranger"), and numerous others.

When men returned home wanting jobs after the war, Kathleen quit the newspaper before she could be let go. In the late 1940s, she took to writing novels.

Gail speaks highly of her mother's fiction. "I have to wonder how they ever made it into [these] magazine[s]," she wrote of Kathleen's love stories in a *New York Times* piece. "They are too complex for the form into which they have been squeezed." She tells me Kathleen's three or four complete novels are wonderful.

But none of the novels ever reached publication. "In spots, she writes like the angels," an editor at Fawcett told

Kathleen's agent. "In others, she hits notes of monstrous tedium calculated to repel the most ardent reader."

A manuscript of Kathleen's novel "The Otherwise Virgins" is designated Series 4.3, Box 75, Folders 963-966, in the Gail Godwin Papers. Actually, it's a joint mother-daughter effort, written by Kathleen and apparently practiced upon by the young Gail. On the cover page is a handwritten note, probably by Gail, reading, "GG's 'first novel'—a rewrite of KK's [Kathleen's] novel."

In the story, Deborah Parrish is a Cardiff College sorority queen, but the arrival on campus of one of her former johns threatens to expose her past as a high-priced call girl and scotch her engagement to Henry Van Storen IV. Scheming freshman Lisa has come to college for the sole purpose of husband hunting, her quarry being Deborah's old client. Breastless, bookish, bespectacled Jane is a minister's daughter with lesbian leanings who vows to turn Lisa on to the life of the mind.

I'm no literary archaeologist, and the librarian announces closing time before I can read as far as I'd like, but I still feel I can distinguish the handiwork of daughter Gail and mother Kathleen. The description of the students' arrival on campus and the capsule account of Deborah's rise from whore to debutante are textured and rich, but the plot points are so familiar that one could take a stab at outlining the novel without reading past page 20.

It's easy to see the influence of the mother who taught, worked for the newspaper, and wrote pulp in her famous daughter who paints, composes librettos, and writes literature.

In *Evensong*, heroine Margaret ultimately repudiates her mother's life by returning home to her husband and raising a daughter of her own.

But some daughters proudly become their mothers and even improve on their legacy.

Evensong isn't the only novel that makes 1999 a blessed year for mountain writers.

As promised, Fred Chappell provides me updates on his progress in writing the novel that is to be called *Look Back All the Green Valley*. He's efficient. Every time I send him a brief written query, I have a response from him in my mailbox in three or four days.

"I've got 3 chapters so far, probably about 75-90 pages," he tells me, and in another letter, "I have a fairly well done Chapter 2 and very rough drafts, almost skeletal in some respects, on 1-5."

These things don't mean much to me, as I don't even know the conceit of the novel. What's of greater interest is the undercurrent of nagging responsibilities. Fred tells me of speaking at a prep school in Delaware; traveling to a booksellers' convention in Mobile; attending a two-day symposium on his own writing; going to a book festival in Nashville; reading poetry for the National Book Award, for which he is a judge; attending the awards ceremony in New York, at which Charles Frazier's *Cold Mountain* is the surprise winner in fiction; writing book reviews for newspapers; reading a novel manuscript for a friend; writing a foreword for a poetry book; preparing lectures for Nichols State University and the Tennessee Williams Literary Festival in New Orleans; writing a commencement address for East Carolina University; writing an inauguration ode for the president of Georgia State University; and speaking at a local middle school. Of course, this is in addition to the duties of his full-time teaching job: leading workshops, reading material by the young men and women in his classes, meeting with students for conferences. I wonder when he shoehorns in work on his novel.

And in the middle of all this comes news that Fred has been named the state's poet laureate. In an article in my local newspaper, he calls it "the friendliest, cheerfulest and most harmless of all state-appointed posts." He might have added "most time-consuming," too.

"My duties were simply to take poetry to different places, mostly give readings, at high schools, grammar schools, community colleges, colleges, churches, libraries—lots of libraries—retirement homes, all kinds of places," he tells me later in his campus office. One of his gigs was writing and reading a poem when President Bill Clinton came to the mountains to designate the New River an American Heritage River.

"Everybody wanted new stuff?" I ask.

"For those things that were just readings, I would take a selection of North Carolina poetry from different people. Sometimes, I'd read my own. The hardest thing was to figure out what the hell they wanted. Anyhow, I was asked to write poems for a number of occasions—the opening of a library, the anniversary of a university or a college, the retirement of somebody from a position. So I wrote lots and lots of occasional poems like that. And I read lots and lots of manuscripts from people."

"That's part of it?"

"That just comes with the territory, I guess. People write a lot of folk poetry and send it to you, and you have to write something nice back."

But here's what surprises me most. "Not a lick of progress," he writes in one letter updating me on *Look Back All the Green Valley*. "Just got in the copy-edited ms. of my translation of Euripides' *Alcestis* and it's in a horrible mess—so, Lord knows when I can get back to the novel."

He translates Greek?

Fred's reticence and modesty make people want to impress him. I remember seeing a few of my fellow graduate students playing erudite with him, telling him everything they'd read and what they'd gleaned from it. Knowing a little about the man, I understood that Fred could polish off their reading lists before breakfast. I listened for a put-down, but it never came. Fred's willing ear and noncommittal nature only made them try harder.

So when I ask him about his translation, I'm on guard against this tendency. I pretend to be indifferent to his accomplishments, inscrutable even. Maybe I've done some Greek translations myself, and I don't need to apologize for them like he does; maybe they're in the folder in my lap even as I sit in his office. Or maybe I know of Euripides but can't recall the name of anything he wrote—aside, now, from *Alcestis*. I could be expert or rube; Fred will never read it in my face.

"I'm guessing the translation is an assignment you sought out, rather than one that sought you out," I venture.

"No, no, no, that's the one I never would have thought of doing in my whole life. *Alcestis* is such a well-known play,

I'm not sure it needs another translation. But a friend of mine was putting together this translation that he had asked for from somebody else, from a real scholar, and it turned out not to be satisfactory, and he asked me as kind of an emergency measure if I could translate *Alcestis* in I think it was about six weeks, or something like that. And I did, but it was a rush job, and I was so uncertain about how to translate from a language I just barely know."

"Have you studied it formally, or are you self-taught?"

"Self-taught. I taught myself some Greek, started back when I was in graduate school. I keep it up a little bit now and then."

"How did he know of your familiarity with the language?" I ask.

"Well, we're old friends. He did a collection of Roman drama, too, and I did a play from Platus for him, which I really enjoyed doing."

He translates Latin, too?

"But this Euripides, because of my uncertain scholarship, turned out to be the dullest translation," he says. "I didn't take any chances whatsoever."

He bad-mouths his laureateship as well.

"The poet who preceded you died during his tenure, didn't he?" I ask.

"He did. It was a lifelong tenure at that time, and they changed it to five years when they got to me. They didn't trust me."

It's hard to tell what effect all of Fred's obligations are having on his writing. He tells me he's done several rewrites on the ending of chapter 2. He indicates in one letter that he's finished the first three chapters and is moving on to rewrites of the next three, then says in the following letter that his opening chapter needs a complete reworking. He takes his manuscript on the road and reads from it publicly at some of his appearances, but what he gleans from this are mainly ideas for further revisions. "But as far as getting forwarder . . . No, alas," he writes.

But maybe this is his usual way of making progress. I remember reading a quote from Fred years ago to the effect that he considers himself an average writer but a first-rate reviser. He apparently goes through several drafts of "handscript" before he ever types his chapters. At no time does a computer seem to enter the process.

There comes a point when it appears he is stalled. "Am looking forward to getting into 5. Lord knows when that might be," he writes.

And then his next letter says this: "My progress report is: no progress. There simply have been no hours for me to work on the book. And there won't be for some five or six weeks."

I decide to give our correspondence a rest. I let the requisite five or six weeks pass, then get lazy and go another seven or eight without querying him. By the time I finally write, his ship has sailed.

"Yes, at last I have a draft of *Look Back All the Green Valley*," he writes.

Movement is quick after that. He mails the novel off; it is accepted by Picador USA; his agent negotiates a deal; a release date is scheduled; his editor asks for revisions; Fred accomplishes those. Our correspondence peters out.

The task he has set himself is complex. The final note in his "octave" of interrelated books, the new novel has narrative and structural obligations to four previous volumes of poetry and three of fiction. "This means that it is top-heavy with theme," Fred tells me, "and that always means you have to struggle sweatily to find a story that can carry so much thematic weight." Moreover, it has to fit a framework that combines ten chapters with a prologue, a "midpiece," and an epilogue. "If the books aren't symmetrically alike, the parallels get lost and the whole edifice is busted," he says. The novel's dominant classical element, earth, must be easily recognizable, so as to echo its companion fourth poetry volume, *Earthsleep*. And its largest theme—the passing away of the mountain culture—must be perceptible. Lastly, the book's many allegiances to the other seven volumes mustn't keep it from standing on its own without reference to its companions, for those readers unfamiliar with the entire cycle.

The titles of all four novels are taken from Appalachian songs. The first, *I Am One of You Forever*, introduces mountain farm boy Jess Kirkman and his close-knit family during the World War II years. The second, *Brighten the Corner Where You Are*, follows a strange day in the life of Jess's father, Joe Robert Kirkman, who must answer for his handling of evolutionary theory in the classroom. In the third, *Farewell, I'm Bound to Leave You*, Jess's mother attends his grandmother on her deathbed while Jess and Joe Robert wait in the next room, where they kill time by remembering the strong women of the family.

Fred is on record as saying that one of his goals is "to

produce a daring and even experimental novel which would not look or feel experimental."

Indeed, the reviewers of his Kirkman books have fallen for their surface simplicity and missed their organizational intricacies, their classical overtones, and their interrelatedness to the *Midquest* poems. Even as late as the third novel, the major reviewers were befuddled. The *New York Times Book Review* called *Farewell, I'm Bound to Leave You* "not quite a novel, but more than a collection of linked short stories." *Booklist* failed to clarify matters in saying it was "actually a set of short stories stitched together into a gallery of idiosyncratic characters." *Library Journal*'s parenthetical approach was weakest of all: "Chappell begins this novel (and although it could appear to be a short story collection, it is a novel, held together by themes, songs, and stories from the past that a young man tries to interpret into the present) with a brilliant death bed set piece."

But they're hardly to blame for missing the finer points of a masterwork twenty-eight years in the making. I certainly didn't understand the overall conception until it was explained to me. Even Fred has been known to blanch at his undertaking. "Better to fail as the clown who wrote the whole thing than as the chicken who didn't," he says.

By the time *Look Back All the Green Valley* is released, news has traveled that it marks the completion of Fred's eight-book opus, and now it seems that readers have known all along that such a work was in the making, and followed it from the start. Lest anyone miss the point, the publisher offers this as the first sentence of its jacket copy: "With *Look Back All the Green Valley*, Fred Chappell brings to a close one of the most rewarding cycles of novels in recent memory."

Fred, too, is quick to reveal his artifice. In the novel's first chapter, Jess Kirkman comes back to the mountains after a twenty-one-year absence. To call his identity transparent is to understate the case. Jess teaches at a university; his mother chides him for his "excessive drinking" and for "writing poetry nobody can understand"; two of his poetry volumes are *River* and *Earthsleep*—the first and last volumes of the *Midquest* cycle—and they were written under the pseudonym Fred Chappell; Jess's wife is Susan, as is Fred's real-life wife, who appears in *Midquest*; Jess is struggling to translate a classic work, in this case *The Divine Comedy*.

Jess's father, Joe Robert, has been dead ten years, and his mother, Cora, is succumbing to congestive heart failure. Jess's return home is occasioned by a mix-up at the cemetery. Having oversold its plots, it has no room for Cora, so Jess and his sister must find a new burial place for their parents. In the process of carrying out his mother's deathbed wishes, Jess uncovers hints of possible marital infidelity on Joe Robert's part, and his effort to solve this new family mystery is the thrust of the novel.

Reviews of the book are positive and readers' reactions appreciative, though the kind of grumblings that have accompanied all the Kirkman books are occasionally heard again—namely, that *Look Back All the Green Valley* is a collection of short stories and not really a novel at all.

In one sense a feat of literary daring, in another an elaborate puzzle, in still another a colossal inside joke, the eight-book cycle is less a commercial success than a rich field for private study for many years to come—which is no doubt the way Fred prefers it.

The biggest success of the year is without question Robert Morgan.

Morgan was raised on a farm near the Green River in Henderson County, south of Asheville. Though his parents had little schooling, they kept a dictionary, a Bible, and a small selection of novels, history books, religious tracts, and *National Geographic*s around the house. In the mornings, he and his mother read Dick and Jane books. In the evenings, Morgan would sit on one of his father's knees and his sister on the other and listen to him read stories.

When in 1958 the Henderson County Bookmobile began stopping at Green River Baptist Church, it was a revelation to Morgan. The bookmobile was nothing grander than an old utility truck fitted with shelves, but it contained the greatest quantity of books the fourteen-year-old had ever seen. He started with Jack London's Klondike tales and James Oliver Curwood's stories of the Royal Canadian Mounties and graduated to *Oliver Twist* and *David Copperfield*. Having seen *War and Peace* advertised in the Sears & Roebuck catalog as "the greatest novel ever written," he was delighted to find it in the rolling library's collection.

Like most mountain farm families, Morgan's was cash-poor. They didn't have money for a car, truck, or tractor and had to borrow a horse when they needed one.

In Morgan's sixth-grade year, his class took a trip to Biltmore House, but he didn't have the three-dollar fee and so had to stay at school. Knowing his liking for Jack London, his teacher suggested he spend the day writing about a man lost in the Canadian Rockies. That was Morgan's first experience writing fiction, and he was surprised how quickly it passed the day. But he didn't really catch fire until he was at North Carolina State studying to be an engineer. When he couldn't get into a math course he wanted, he enrolled in a fiction-writing class. He subsequently transferred to the University of North Carolina for his bachelor's, got an MFA, and landed a position teaching writing at Cornell while still a young man, quite a rise from his modest roots.

His publication record was steady, if unspectacular—nine volumes of poetry, a pair of short-story collections, and two novels. His first poetry collection was published by Russell Banks, a friend and classmate at Chapel Hill. Morgan's second novel, *The Truest Pleasure*, was selected a *Publishers Weekly* Best Book of the Year and a *New York Times* Notable Book.

Ask anyone who's met him and they'll tell you Morgan is one of the nicest guys in the business. He always finds time to give readings and to autograph. He's gracious and humble. He respects serious writing, good or bad. He never complains to his publisher about marketing, publicity, accommodations, or meals.

That said, it's doubtful his characters would find him such a fine fellow.

In his 1999 novel, *Gap Creek*, he creates for his narrator, Julie Harmon, a string of misfortunes that would make Job quail. Gail Godwin's *Evensong* is set at the cusp of the millennium; some of her characters, afraid of the apocalypse, are apprehensive about crossing the threshold.

Gap Creek is set a hundred years earlier, at the doorstep of the twentieth century, and it seems the modern age can't come quickly enough for the mountain people.

The novel opens with Julie's younger brother burning with fever from a mysterious illness. She and her father bring him down the mountain, taking turns carrying him in their arms, to the doctor in Flat Rock. On the return slog, Julie is toting him when he coughs up a bellyful of white worms and strangles to death. Her father isn't long for this world either, dying of consumption in the second chapter and leaving Julie to do the backbreaking work for what is now a houseful of women.

Rescue comes in the person of dark-haired, stoutly built Hank Richards, who marries Julie and takes her across the South Carolina border to live in a rented home in Gap Creek. Julie's duty is to care for the home's owner, a crusty widower named Pendergast. One day, while rendering fat on the stove, she sets the house on fire. Pendergast is badly burned while trying to save his pension money and dies a short time later.

The house is only slightly damaged, and the young couple's fortunes seem to be on the rise, as Julie is newly pregnant and she and Hank now have free run of the place and a jar of found money. But a fast-talking stranger bilks Julie out of the money, and Hank loses his job at the cotton mill. Gap Creek floods, carries away the chicken coop, and drowns their only cow. Julie delivers her baby all alone and nearly dies afterward; her premature daughter, in fact, does.

At the close of the novel, Pendergast's heirs announce their intention to claim the house. Hank and Julie, pregnant again, must return on foot to North Carolina, their only possessions what they can carry over the mountains in their arms.

All this, and Julie is only seventeen.

Gap Creek is released in September 1999, and the publisher, Algonquin Books of Chapel Hill, is pleased to sell through the ten-thousand-copy print run over the holidays.

Morgan receives a phone call in early January. "It was a woman," he tells me later. "She said, 'I picked up your book and couldn't put it down. It says on the back of the novel that *Gap Creek* is the work of a master' "—Fred Chappell's jacket blurb—" 'and that's really true.' "

"She didn't tell you who she was?" I ask.

"No. She said, 'I have a little book club, and I'd like you to come and speak to us.' I thought it was a lady I had met from South Carolina. I told her I'd be glad to speak to her group, though I really didn't know when I'd be able to get down there. And then later in the conversation, she said she was in Chicago, and it began to dawn on me."

Oprah Winfrey likes to call authors personally, dust off her Southern accent, and have a little fun with them. *Gap Creek* is the twenty-ninth selection of her book club, she finally gets around to telling Morgan.

Algonquin also receives a call. "I can remember every moment of all of it," Morgan's editor, Duncan Murrell, tells me later. "I remember sitting at my desk, and I forget who took the phone call, but we were informed by Oprah's people that *Gap Creek* would be selected. This process all started happening on a Monday evening. They called late. And one of the stipulations was that we weren't to call Robert right away, because Oprah was in the middle of trying to find him."

One problem is that the show's producer would like five copies immediately for staff use. A modest second printing is in the works, but for the time being, the well is dry; Algonquin has only three copies in house. And then Oprah wants five hundred copies to distribute to her audience the following week, when she will publicly declare the selection of *Gap Creek*.

"It would be announced the following Tuesday, I think, and this was a Monday, which was an extraordinarily short period of time," Murrell says. "That wasn't the typical amount of time that she gave. I'm not sure why. In any case, we were all very, very excited about it. But there wasn't a lot of time to be excited, and to jump up and down and celebrate and pop champagne, because there was only a week to get it done. And getting it done meant there were hundreds of thousands of books we had to print to get out there initially. And it meant going to the printers and convincing them to shuck off everything else they were working on and crank these things out."

"Was all of this a matter of contract with the *Oprah* show?" I ask.

"There was a contract signed with Oprah. There were a lot of rules that she had."

"Regarding secrecy before she announced the book?"

"Everything from secrecy to how the *Oprah* logo was to be displayed. We were presented with an array of logos that you could use on the cover of the book. What size and all that was all dictated by her. This was all work very happily done, by the way. I'm not complaining. But you had to very quickly produce a reader's guide that could be put on the website, and an author biography."

One of Algonquin's responsibilities is making travel arrangements for Morgan.

"They brought me down and filmed me walking along Gap Creek," Morgan tells me. "They also filmed me at my grandmother's grave site." Julie Harmon is loosely based on his maternal grandmother, Julia Capps Levi.

The staff manages to scrounge the five copies for the producer but has to prevail upon a major book distributor to gather the five hundred audience copies without leaking the news, and then to overnight them to Chicago.

Meanwhile, Algonquin orders a printing of 350,000 copies, which, impossibly, must be in stores by the time Oprah makes her announcement a week hence. When orders for the book reach 600,000, Algonquin orders a third printing before the second is done. Of course, since secrecy must be maintained while the announcement is pending, bookstores don't even know what they're ordering. They're not buying Robert Morgan's *Gap Creek*, but rather Oprah's new selection, sight unseen.

"It took a herculean effort to get it done," Murrell says. "The other thing was that there was a holiday. The Martin Luther King holiday intervened between the Monday that she told us and the Tuesday that it was to be announced, and when those books were supposed to be in the stores. Nobody worked on Monday, so everything had to be done by Sunday, and shipping by Tuesday, so we did a lot of funny things, interesting things, like shipping books in waves as they were coming off the press. One chain sent their own trucks to the press just so they could take them straight off the press to the bookstores. It was a very exciting time, that's for sure.

"After it was announced, of course, it was just great to see Robert get a lot of press."

It's long afterward when I finally acquire a tape of Oprah's *Gap Creek* book-club installment. Like most people in the industry, I rue the day Jonathan Franzen famously criticized Oprah's low-culture approach and declined to be on her program. Many of her selections brought credit to worthy authors who otherwise would have labored in obscurity their entire careers. And she pumped money into a flagging industry. Everyone in the business reaped benefits from the show, directly or indirectly.

But when I finally sit down to watch the program, I understand Franzen's point. Robert Morgan, the guest of honor, doesn't even make an appearance until it's past the halfway point. Instead, the discussion centers around modern conveniences. Oprah reports the percentages of people who say they couldn't live without tampons, deodorant, panty hose, hair spray, television, and cell phones. To everyone's great delight, one newly married young man pipes up from the audience that it's condoms he would miss most. All of this is far removed from Julie Harmon in her upstate South Carolina cabin. All told, the author gets maybe three minutes of air time. When questions arise concerning Appalachian culture, they're referred not to Morgan, who grew up in the mountains and has spent his entire adult life writing about them, but to a crackerjack hired-gun expert, that old-time backwoods gal Rory Kennedy, daughter of Robert F. Kennedy. Her principal contribution is to give the opinion that—surprise!—little has changed in the Appalachians in the last hundred years. It's pretty lightweight stuff.

But you'll never hear it from Morgan, even if he feels that way, which I doubt.

Duncan Murrell tells me of a conversation one of his Algonquin colleagues had with the author. "She was on the phone with him, and she got the impression that he didn't really realize how many copies of the book would be produced. So she said to him, 'Robert, we're printing two or three hundred thousand copies of this book.' And he had apparently told his wife, when she asked what it meant, 'Oh, I think maybe it'll be another twenty or thirty thousand copies of the book.' So he was off by an order of ten. And it wasn't one of those things where he was ignorant of Oprah Winfrey or didn't care, it was just that his head was not wrapped up in those numbers. You can find writers out there who could have told you right off the top of their head how many copies being picked by Oprah means, but Robert's not one of them."

In all languages and editions, there are two million copies of *Gap Creek* in print today. The only downside to the experience, Morgan tells me, is the prospect of sales for his next novel. "Afterward, it's kind of hard going back to selling fifty thousand copies of a book."

"I remember driving home one day in the month prior to the show airing," Murrell says. "Once the show airs, then you're no longer the belle of the ball, but for that month, it's just magic.

"So I'm driving home, and I'm listening to NPR, and I forget which of the anchors Robert was talking with, but he was being interviewed on the national show. And I remember the guy asking him something about the money. You know, 'What's it like, now that you're going to be rich?' or something to that effect.

"And Bob says, I can remember this, he says, 'I don't know about that. I'm fifty-six years old. I'm pretty set in my ways—you know, my home. And I don't think there's much that I'm going to do special. But I never thought that I would have so many readers.' "

CHAPTER 7

Night Sweats/Self-Gratification

My plan is to subscribe to Asheville's daily paper, the *Citizen-Times*. I will begin reading it instead of my local rag, and thereby immerse myself in mountain people, places, issues, and events.

But my order is processed incorrectly, and only the Sunday issues show up in my mailbox. They generally arrive on Thursday. Finding I am more wedded to timely news than I thought, I continue reading my local daily. Examining the Asheville paper thus becomes a supplemental chore. The investment of time proves burdensome.

My solution is to clean out a drawer of my dresser and store the Asheville papers there until I have a chance to read them. When that drawer fills, I take the papers out and pile them on the floor in front of the dresser. A knee-high stack grows, then a second beside it. When my wife complains, I spend a couple of hours stripping the papers of everything I never intend to read anyway—advertising circulars, coupons, comics, want ads, business page, auto page, real-estate guide—which leaves only the front section, the local section, sports, and arts and entertainment. I then have a single stack of manageable proportions. I transfer it to the master bathroom, which I keep in such deplorable condition that my wife long ago moved into the bath down the hall with our daughters. I empty the hamper and put the papers in there, making a place for my dirty clothes on the floor between the hamper and the bathtub. Watching the unread papers burgeon has by now become a pastime. Though I strip the new papers upon their arrival, the stack climbs the entire height of the hamper, then grows out the top so that the lid stays permanently open. At this point, my wife tells me I'm eccentric.

I eventually cancel the subscription. The papers, still mainly unread, find their way into a twenty-gallon plastic storage container in the crawlspace, and the clothes go back into the hamper.

So it is with all the background material I accumulate. I buy books on Asheville history and titles by writers connected to the area. What I can't find new I track down through rare-book dealers. Not knowing how many John Ehle or Ann B. Ross titles I ought to read—or whether those authors will consent to an interview, or even whether I'll need them in the book at all—I strive to collect their complete works. I completely fill a bookcase; I stop counting at two hundred titles.

Meanwhile, there are magazine articles, free local weeklies, tourist brochures, maps, correspondence, and such.

These go into the dresser drawer where the newspapers once found a home. As for titles too obscure for even the rare-book dealers, I track them down in libraries and photocopy them complete. These, too, go into the dresser. I fill one drawer, then a second, then ultimately a third, culling and consolidating my underwear, socks, and T-shirts to make room.

I haven't a prayer of digesting all this stuff. Every book I read seems to recommend three or four others; the more I do, the farther behind I get. What I really need is to move to Asheville for a year and live the local culture, but that's not going to happen. My opportunities for writing are limited to Saturdays, Sundays, and weeknights after the kids are in bed and the house is tidied up, which is generally around ten.

Though I hold a regular job and haven't missed a day in fifteen years for reasons other than funerals and my kids' illnesses, people often ask my wife if I'm a stay-at-home dad. Perhaps their observation has merit, even if they're wrong on the facts. I live a protracted adolescence for the sake of writing a book that may never see print and may attract few readers even if it does.

And then there's middle age. I develop a scalp condition characterized by angry pimples all over the back of my head that burn like fire. With it comes dandruff so severe that I can shake my head and watch it fall like snow. The dermatologist advises me to start washing my hair with tar-based bar soap. On the way out of his office, I pick up a brochure on my condition. As is the custom in such literature, the picture on the front shows a victim with what must be the worst case of the disorder in recorded history; he looks a good deal like Norman Mailer but has what appears to be thick white moss growing profusely from his ears. I buy tar-based soap, which costs eight dollars a bar. The good news is that it will last forever, since it won't give up any lather no matter how long and hard it is rubbed. I switch to a popular dandruff shampoo, which corrects the problem within a couple of weeks.

There are other indignities, too. My hair is overtaken by white; my pants strain to popping, as I refuse to go up a waist size; I grow tits. But the worst trouble is my eyes. I do close reading all day at work off a computer screen, then come home and read into the night. Some mornings when I wake, I have pain in one or the other of my eyes so sharp that I can't hold it open. It might be five minutes before I can begin to use the eye, which remains sensitive to touch, light, and any breath of moving air throughout the day. It is more often the right eye than the left but has never been both on the same morning. I assure myself it's muscle cramping, the result of holding a short-distance focus for extended periods, though that's largely a guess. I don't really want to know for sure, not until I get my book written.

The writers' group meeting begins with someone reading a brief communication from Jack Pyle and Taylor Reese, who are wintering in Florida. They have an autographing scheduled for next month, when they'll be back in the mountains.

Next, Terri, the group's president, circulates a magazine article entitled "First Fiction Highlights" and reads an e-mail from Linda Worth, a poet who has attended only one of our meetings but wants to remain in touch nonetheless. Linda reports that she is a regular at open-mike nights at her favorite chain bookstore, that she's had a poem accepted by a literary magazine at a community college—her first success—and that she is being mentored in her writing by a neighbor who is a retired English teacher. She wants to make it to more of our meetings—*mettings*, actually, as I see when I obtain a copy of her missive. Linda hopes we haven't forgotten her.

I am traveling to the writers' group less frequently as time passes. It is hard to motivate myself to get up at six-thirty on a Saturday morning and make a six-hour round-trip drive for the sake of a two-hour meeting. This particular Saturday, I am the scribe of the monthly minutes, which I will take home, type up, and submit for mailing to all the members. Bryan Aleksich has recently joined the group, but he's not present today.

It seems to me that the tone of the proceedings has changed. The husband and wife who ran the meetings when I started coming have together survived a house fire and separately suffered back surgery and an auto accident. They no longer attend. And one of my favorite members, retired professor Gerald Gullickson—a monument to endurance who once published six hundred poems in fly-by-night magazines in the span of two years—has died. We seldom read from our work anymore. And the complaining about agents and editors seems more strident.

Since the members still see me primarily as a representative of the industry, rather than a fellow writer, I am saddled with a small share of the blame for the state of publishing, or so I feel. This is especially true since my company rejected manuscripts by several members.

"Don't you find that to be the case, Steve?" I might hear, after a discussion of the misspellings rampant in commercial books.

Or "Have you seen any of that at your company, Steve?" following a lament about midlist authors having their contracts dropped by publishers.

I shouldn't overstate the case. But I sense an undercurrent.

After reading the communication from Linda Worth, Terri, the president, tells how she's been working twelve-hour days lately, and so has little time to write. She is awaiting word on a novel submission to a publisher out west.

The lady next to her reports that she has two novels being handled by two different agents. Those agents have supposedly received positive comments from publishers but no offers.

The lady next to her describes the travel articles and the memoir she is writing and passes around a pamphlet about the Kentucky Book Fair.

Next is an elderly gentleman working on a manuscript about a one-eyed Scottish terrier.

Joanne reads what she calls a "bug poem," which proves to be exactly what it claims. She says parents and kids love them, though she has had no luck getting them published.

Suzanne says she is putting together a song collection. I wasn't aware we did songs.

Caroline is waiting to hear the results of a contest in which she's entered a novel manuscript.

Nancy, one of our guests this day, is writing a memoir in her mother's voice.

Jonathan, our other guest, is working on a novel and some short stories. He says he used to write screenplays and television scripts. He once made a living writing continuity—the bridges between segments—for old television programs like *The Tennessee Ernie Ford Show*.

A good portion of the meeting is given over to a discussion of Bill Brooks, a local community-college instructor and author of commercial Westerns.

Cynthia tells how she was recently devastated by Brooks's critique of her work in a writing class of his. The substance of his comments never comes quite clear in the telling, though one of the principal points seems to be Brooks's judgment that her novel needs more "layering." Cynthia comes back to the word several times.

It is quickly apparent that the man has a reputation. A couple of members hasten to Cynthia's defense.

Steve Brown was skewered in a Bill Brooks class when he turned in a portion of one of his mystery novels.

"Don't ever try to write first-person in a man's voice," Brooks once scolded longtime member Vickie. "You just can't pull it off."

Other sympathetic voices join in.

There isn't a thing wrong with Cynthia's writing, someone says.

Cynthia writes simple, straightforward, old-fashioned, good stories.

Just because they're simple on the surface doesn't mean they lack depth.

The consensus seems to be that Bill Brooks is a good writer and an experienced teacher, but that he ought to be more sensitive in his criticism.

There's nothing to be gained by making things personal.

He's a skilled writer, all right, but he shouldn't try to evaluate work outside his genre.

The purpose of a critique is to point out areas for improvement, not to tear someone down.

Virginia, a soft-spoken elderly woman, is currently taking a class from Brooks. The students must turn in a love scene. Since two of the characters in her novel-in-progress are homosexuals, she has tried her hand at putting gay love on the page. She hasn't heard back from Brooks but is now beginning to worry, she tells us.

Everyone gets a laugh out of that.

"Good luck," someone says.

"Better buckle your chin strap, dear."

So that's the way I report it in the minutes when I get home. I summarize the members' various writings, submissions, contest entries, and conference experiences, but my longest paragraph is devoted to Bill Brooks. Never having met the man, I chide him for his harshness toward student work, which I tie to his being a rough-and-tumble Western feller. I laud those who would challenge his notions with scenes of gay couplings. I understand the group's minutes to be of the character of in-house memos, so I feel confident in expressing myself freely. I believe I'm defending the wronged. I also think what I write is kind of clever.

It appears I'm mistaken.

During my few years of sporadically attending meetings, only a couple of people have made themselves unwelcome. One was a poetry-writing hard case of a mountain man who, the first time someone tried to inquire about his work, answered, "I write what I write. You think you can do better?" He never came back. Others have been openly critical of the group's commercial orientation, which hasn't helped their popularity.

I send the minutes to Terri, who photocopies and mails them.

A few days after that, a separate mailing arrives from Cynthia.

"This is in response to the minutes of the recent meeting," it begins. "I feel my remarks concerning Bill Brooks were taken out of context."

Cynthia says she has enjoyed her instruction from Brooks and hopes to enroll in more of his classes in the future. While it is true that he said her work would benefit from more layering, she feels his remarks were delivered in the spirit of helpfulness.

She would never seek to criticize Brooks or any other fellow writer, she says.

It goes on for a full page.

I call Cynthia to apologize. She says she bears me no ill will; she wrote her letter when her feelings were running high; indeed, she's been worried she offended *me*.

I also call Steve Brown, who says he doesn't know what the big deal is, that I just reported things as they happened.

I also call Jack Pyle, who wasn't at the meeting but is a pretty good judge of fairness. He is surprised at Cynthia's follow-up; it looks to him like I was pretty straightforward. But of course, he can't say for sure.

I appreciate the support, though I suspect Steve and Jack are being nice. I really don't know what my future reception at the writers' group will be.

Self-publishing liberates the group's members.

Eileen Johnson, a sharp-dressing, well-spoken woman in her seventies, is the first to drag a toe in the water. Eileen and her husband, a retired naval officer, spent six years traveling through every state in the country in their motor home before settling in the North Carolina mountains. They live in Old Fort, located at the base of the last big push up the Blue Ridge to Asheville. The building of the railroad westward from Old Fort by convict laborers in the 1870s is the subject of *The Road*, John Ehle's classic novel. That monumental effort opened Asheville to the outside world. You're unlikely to travel that same six-mile grade via Interstate 40 today without passing a few broken-down vehicles unable to make it to the top.

After her move to North Carolina, Eileen began taking trips to Ireland, the land of her ancestry. Struck by the many parallels in folklore, dance, music, and crafts between Ireland and the southern Appalachians—attributable to the Scots-Irish migration of the nineteenth century—she resolved to write a book on the subject.

When it comes time to see her manuscript into print, Eileen doesn't even consider submitting to agents or commercial publishers. "Going through an agent, even in a best-case scenario, it might be three or four years before I could hold that book in my hand," she says. "And besides that, I'd have to go through all the aggravation."

She contacts eighteen or twenty companies that advertise themselves as book printers, only to find that many of them deal mainly in stationery and wedding invitations and merely dabble in books on the side.

She finally learns that the best friend of self-publishing writers resides in Nebraska, a company with a 250,000-square-foot plant devoted exclusively to short-run book production of two hundred to five thousand copies. Those interested can obtain a free kit that exhaustively details the company's many options relating to cover design, photographic reproduction, typefaces, page counts, paper stock, bindings, proofs, shrink-wrapping, shipment, and many other things, along with all the itemized costs pertaining thereto. For a fee, the company's designers will provide as much assistance as the writer desires. Other fees are levied for acquiring an International Standard Book Number, creating a bar code, and filing with the Library of Congress. The company can also supply counter displays and print postcards, bookmarks, brochures, and posters advertising the book. Its sales pitch to writers focuses on its two- to three-month turnaround time, the high degree of control its customers retain over design, production, and sales, and the 40 to 400 percent profit realized by some of the books it prints.

Eileen titles her effort *More Than Blarney: The Irish Influence in Appalachia*, creates her own imprint—Wolfhound Press—and, given her subject matter, publishes under her maiden name, Eileen McCullough.

By the time the book comes out, she has traveled to numerous seminars on Irish subjects and procured address lists of her fellow attendees. Her initial sales are to these people, whom she targets by direct mail. In peddling her book, she much prefers speaking to Friends of the Library organizations and appearing at storytelling festivals and book fairs to signing in bookstores.

Her book is sold in scattered outlets in the mountains and, to her great pleasure, in a couple of stores in Ireland, but truth be told, it is available at relatively few places. Still, she is well satisfied with the venture. She clears enough profit from her thirty-five-hundred-dollar investment in a thousand copies of *More Than Blarney* to finance the printing of another book and to pay for a couple more trips to Ireland. She wishes only that she had hired an editor to catch some of the errors that leaked into the book.

It is Jack Pyle and Taylor Reese who spread the self-publishing fever. Having already written a pair of gardening books for a small commercial publisher, they have in place a network of bookstore and gift-shop contacts throughout the mountains.

In quick succession, Jack underwrites the publication of a couple of mysteries—the second of which is *The Sound of Distant Thunder*, which he once submitted to my company—then a novel called *After Many a Summer*, then a large-print collection of short stories, all through the same Nebraska printer Eileen discovered, all in the company's standard 5½-by-8½ paperback format. Meanwhile, Taylor puts out two collections of homespun humor and a memoir of his boyhood.

All of this enhances their attractiveness to groups looking for speakers. Counting their gardening books, they now have their own mini-store of nine titles. If a person who stops at their table doesn't like mysteries, he or she might be receptive to humor or short stories. Like Eileen, they keep their expectations realistic—Jack contracts mainly for print runs of two thousand copies—and realize a satisfactory profit. They are persuasive spokesmen for controlling one's own fate, rather than praying for the kindness of commercial publishers.

In Jack and Taylor's wake come self-published historical novels, memoirs, mysteries, a young-adult novel, travel narratives, an account of spiritual awakening dedicated to Buddha, *Grandpa Stories, Earth's Only Paradise*, a book boasting an improbable back-cover endorsement from Desmond Tutu, and others.

Spirits run high. High jinks abound.

In the absence of any book reviews to draw from, and having few contacts in the publishing industry, the members write blurbs for each other's work.

"A delightful new series character has been born . . . sure to make a hit with mystery fans," Jack Pyle writes for a friend's book.

That friend returns the favor, calling Jack's first mystery, *The Death of Adam Stone*, "a tense tale that will keep you snatching at pages right up to the surprising end."

Jack releases *The Death of Adam Stone* under Eileen Johnson's imprint, Wolfhound Press. When one reviewer gives the opinion that the book should have been rewritten, Jack writes back on Wolfhound stationery, says the magazine could stand some editing itself, and signs his letter Lenore Johnson, one of Eileen's aliases.

Our undisputed king of self-publishing is Steve Brown.

Steve makes the trip to Asheville from Greenville, South Carolina, and so is the second-farthest-traveled member of the group, after me. He is the kind of person I normally don't like—loud, opinionated, driven. Then again, he is kindhearted and protective of those in need. Among all the members, Steve is the person most welcoming of guests and is always the first to leap to the defense of anyone verbally challenged by the group, as he did for me on one occasion.

An Alabama native, Steve was a combat platoon leader in Vietnam and later worked in sales. At the time I met him, he had been writing novels for fifteen years but had never published a single word. He spoke freely of mystery greats like Raymond Chandler and John D. MacDonald, of big advances and movie deals, as if he were a member of the club, but it was easy to sense his frustration.

In the end, all it took was a serious conversation with Jack Pyle, who told him he could continue standing on one side of the table with the book-buying public, or he could move to the other side and sit with the authors. If there was no one willing to publish his stuff, and if he really believed in it, he should assume the burden himself.

Steve's first self-published novel is *Of Love & War*, a story of the Japanese attack on Pearl Harbor. Following that comes *Color Her Dead*, a mystery starring Myrtle Beach lifeguard and part-time finder of runaways Susan Chase. Next is *Black Fire*, a literary novel set in Alabama, and then *Stripped to Kill*, a second Susan Chase mystery. All appear under Steve's imprint, Chick Springs Publishing, coined from Chick Springs Plantation in *Black Fire*.

The last page of *Black Fire* is followed by an excerpt from its proposed prequel, "Black Funk." *Color Her Dead* has a free excerpt from *Stripped to Kill*, which in turn features both an excerpt from a third Susan Chase mystery and an interview with Steve Brown.

Steve possesses a flair for garnering blurbs—quotes touting a book's merits, usually featured on the back cover. He asks me to write one for *Of Love & War*, and I oblige. But when the book comes out, my quote is nowhere to be found, though there are four others on the back cover, one on the front, and twenty-four inside, before the title page. They come mostly from World War II veterans but also from people identified as bookstore managers, professors of history, ministers, doctors, attorneys, retirees, secretaries, students, teachers, and writers. By *Color Her Dead*, he is getting quotes from published authors.

At one of the writers' group meetings, I sing the praises of Charles Price and the novel of his I've edited. Steve asks me for Charles's address so he can solicit a quote for *Black Fire*. Charles has mixed feelings about the matter and so writes an endorsement he feels won't be used. *Black Fire*, he says, is "crowded with incident" and reads "like an action-movie scenario." Steve runs it prominently.

By his fifth book—*Radio Secrets*, a stalker novel—he no longer needs to ask for quotes, as he is able to use review excerpts from publications as mighty as *Library Journal* and *Booklist*.

Always a popular man among the group, Steve blossoms

into a hero for the downtrodden unpublished. There is an air of excitement when he blows into the room. His absence is publicly regretted during those sessions when he has obligations elsewhere.

He talks of his editor in North Carolina, his artists in Asheville and Dallas, his printer in Michigan. He shows off the plastic table tents he sets up for his book signings. "Myrtle Beach Mysteries," one of them reads. "Suspense," "Southern Gothic," and "Pearl Harbor" are the others. He brings his color-coded index cards bearing the names of bookstore contacts from Asheville to Atlanta. He tells about the legwork he does in advance of each of his autographings. He describes the bumper sticker on his car, which advertises his Susan Chase website, not to be confused with his Chick Springs Publishing website. Visitors to those sites can see Steve's schedule of autographings and read a chapter from each of his novels, chapters from a couple of books not yet published, and a complete novella, *In the Fast Lane*, which is dedicated to Stephen King.

In the span of eighteen months, he puts out six novels and sells twelve thousand copies. *Of Love & War* goes into a second printing of two thousand copies and *Color Her Dead* into a third.

As far as I know, his overarching ambitions are still to be picked up by a New York house and to get a movie contract. If he remains a distance from those goals, he is at least closer than he was.

At last word, Steve has been approached by a couple of writers about publishing under the Chick Springs imprint. He is working out an arrangement whereby he would collect a consulting fee for guiding them through the entire self-publishing process. They would pay all costs—which Steve estimates at eight thousand to ten thousand dollars per title—and ship the books from their own homes, just as he does.

The total of self-published works by members quickly reaches thirty. I purchase most of these and read a good many.

There are some well-written gems and several handsomely designed volumes among them, but most can be identified as self-published from a distance of fifty feet. The cover design is below commercial quality, as is the interior layout. The prose, notwithstanding the editorial help the members have sought out and paid for, is in need of editing. I have a book that begins with "Chapter 1" and continues with "Chapter Two," and in which the odd-numbered pages are on the right for the first half of the story, as they should be, and on the left for the remainder. I have another that begins at the top of page 2 in the middle of a sentence. Page 1 is profoundly blank, as are pages 4, 5, 8, 9, 12, 13, 16, 17, and 20, which gets the book off to a rather rocky start. All of this serves to reaffirm my belief in industry standards.

Then again, the big houses are not above putting out shoddy stuff, as everyone laments. Commercially published books—including my own—have plenty of embarrassing gaffes. And proofreading is a lost art even in the works of major authors.

The members have struggled at their desks as long as the pros, and they put greater effort into marketing their wares.

So why shouldn't they have a place at the banquet?

I drive an aged red Ford with an oil leak. Every time it downshifts going uphill, I expect it to leave its transmission on the pavement. It has a hole in its muffler. The steering makes noise. Worst is its worn-out wiring, which sometimes causes it to stall. I've spent a few hundred dollars on diagnostic tests to pin down this latter problem, only to be told that the car will likely have to fail completely before the defect can be identified.

The Ford has always responded to coddling if I need something special from it, as now, when I'm driving to Asheville. I overfill the oil, pour a container of leak-slowing chemical in the crankcase, fill the tank with premium-grade gas, and drive it through the automatic carwash.

It runs loudly but well the first hour in the rolling country through Statesville and Hickory. As I begin to climb past Morganton to Marion, traffic comes to a halt in a construction zone. Without air hitting the radiator, the engine heats up and the fan comes noisily to life. I can see and smell a light breath of oil smoke.

I've not slept well in my own bed lately, but slumber comes easily when I'm behind the wheel. Lukewarm root beer is my stimulant of choice. I pop open my second one of the afternoon.

The occasion is a party for several members of the writers' group, who will be giving a joint discussion of their newly self-published books at the main public library in Asheville. The principal attraction is Jack Pyle. Jack suffered a heart attack on Halloween and underwent double bypass

surgery shortly thereafter. It is now less than two weeks before Christmas, and his first public venture, to no one's surprise, will be to promote his book and to speak for the
broader cause of writing. Eileen Johnson will be presenting, too. The event is judged to be of such moment that the
group has canceled its regular monthly meeting in an effort
to encourage people to attend the party. That really wasn't
necessary, as all the members without obligations are sure
to come. I hope my own effort in making the drive will help
soothe any bad feelings I may have created with the Bill
Brooks flap, but mainly I just want to enjoy the company
and to hear what the speakers have to say.

I put down my root beer when traffic starts moving
again.

If I have mixed feelings about their self-publishing ventures, I also acknowledge that they've accomplished more
than I have lately. I've saved two weeks of vacation at the
end of the year to work on my book. Unfortunately, I am
presently editing a restaurant guide containing some two
hundred and forty eateries. I find myself with fifty-three
entries to go and only three scheduled working days. My
most optimistic projections leave me with twenty entries to
edit over Christmas. I'll also have to edit the contents page,
the acknowledgments, the general introduction, and the six
smaller introductions to the various sections of the book.
Then I'll need to spell-check the files and enter all the
author's corrections. Meanwhile, my own project will languish, I'll be surly at family occasions over the holidays, and
I'll continue sleepless.

Despite its faults, the Ford is the best mountain climber

I've ever owned. It maintains an effortless sixty on the big hill up from Old Fort, where greater vehicles fail.

From the edge of my vision, I note the temperature gauge rising and the dashboard lights popping on one by one: SEATBELT, DOOR AJAR, WATER, SERVICE ENGINE SOON, OIL.

It seems to run better when it's all lit up.

CHAPTER 8

Ham-and-Eggers

I'm riding a bus with my daughter's fifth-grade class.
I'm chaperoning a field trip to a science museum an hour
away.

I've just begun reading a romance novel, *Essence of My
Desire* by Jill Jones. On its hot-pink cover is an antique perfume bottle. In the center of the bottle, an inch-square
peekaboo cutaway reveals a bouquet of flowers on the first
interior page. After that comes a page with capsule raves
from publications called *Affaire de Coeur*, *Romantic Times*,
and *Belles and Beaux of Romance*.

The story begins in New Orleans as Simone Lefèvre receives a mysterious package containing an unidentified perfume. The daughter of the late master perfumer Jean René
Lefèvre, Simone has fallen on hard times since Englishman
Nick Rutledge, her first lover, stole her father's secret for-
mulas and left town. Meanwhile, in London, Nick Rutledge,

too, takes delivery of a strange perfume. Like Simone, Nick has seen his fortunes slide. Crafty Frenchman Antoine Dupuis tricked him into his theft of Jean René Lefèvre's life's work, then gained control of Nick's family's perfume empire, the House of Rutledge.

An ocean apart, Simone and Nick test the perfume and find it has a highly erotic effect. In their dreams, they are transported to a land of indigo mist and an hour of sizzling passion with . . . each other!

Simone is enraged; Nick Rutledge is her sworn enemy.

Nick is tormented; he is ashamed of his duplicity toward Simone.

Before long, Simone receives an invitation from Antoine Dupuis to come to London to interview for a position at the House of Rutledge. In England, she rents a cottage on a country estate. It is, she learns, the former home of a witch and the place where her mysterious perfume was concocted. Meanwhile, Nick decides to take a weekend at his country estate, where he has just begun renting out an old cottage to bring in some needed cash. He parks his Triumph roadster, saddles his Arabian stallion to go introduce himself to his new renter at the cottage, knocks on the door, and—

"Enjoying your book?"

It's the lady in the seat in front of me, another of the chaperons. She's been bending the teacher's ear up to this point and has apparently worn her out.

"Book?" I say.

"Are you enjoying your book?"

"It's okay."

I go back to reading.

"Is it something for work?"

"No, I wouldn't say that."

She's not accustomed to having her curiosity go unsatisfied, I can tell. Her daughter is the star of the class, and that ought to command a certain amount of deference from someone like me. She's turned sideways. I catch her looking over the seat every now and then, trying to see what it is I'm reading. I have to tilt the top edge down until the book is flat across my leg.

She finally leaves me alone—until we pull up outside the museum.

"What's that you're reading?"

I pretend I don't hear.

"What's that you're reading?"

"Uh, nothing."

That answer, so flagrantly false, stuns her long enough for me to slip past, tucking the book in the inside pocket of my jacket, where it will stay until I can continue in peace.

I ask Jill Jones how it feels to be a moneymaker for the publishing industry and yet to be disparaged by many book people for being a genre author. I ask how it feels to be denied the luxury of writer's block but to be criticized for spewing formula stuff on a tight schedule. I want to know what it's like to be a guilty pleasure to people like me.

"Here's my answer," she says. "Show me the money. Genre writers make more money than literary writers, and I am not embarrassed to be a genre writer. And no, we don't get the literary accolades and all that kind of thing, but it doesn't matter to me. I have people who write me wonderful fan letters, saying things like, 'I was sick and I read your book, and it took my mind off my worries,' or 'You entertained me. You kept me up all night.' Those are the good words. Those are my critics.

"First of all, I don't get reviewed in a lot of the highbrow magazines, so that's not an issue. I feel like I'm in the entertainment business. I'm not necessarily in the literature business. And if I write a story that keeps people up at night and keeps them turning pages, then I'm entertaining them. That's the same as somebody who's on TV or somebody who's in the movies. It's just a different medium."

Jill lives in Montreat, east of Asheville, where she works part-time as an administrator for the Swannanoa Valley Museum. Her husband owns a travel agency and is a gourmet chef and a cookbook author. Jill enjoys house painting and home restoration. Indeed, I catch her with cement on her hands when I reach her by phone. She's been laying tile.

Born in Oklahoma, she grew up in the oil patches of Texas and Louisiana. After earning a degree in journalism and professional writing, she worked for fifteen years in advertising—"the ultimate fiction," she calls it. It was after that when her thoughts turned to the possibilities of love.

"I joined the Romance Writers of America, at the recommendation of a friend who was a romance writer wannabe," she says. "I went to one of their conferences, and I didn't even know what the romance genre was at the time. There were eight hundred people there, and they were among the most professional writers I'd ever met. These were 99 percent women. The guest speaker was Mary

Higgins Clark, and the luncheon guest speaker was LaVyrle Spencer, and it was kind of an eye-opener for me.

"And so then I joined an RWA chapter. I had a critique group, and I was very lucky, because I was the only unpublished writer in the whole group, so I had a lot of mentors."

Jill's writing breakthrough came while she was working on a manuscript with a reincarnation theme. She happened to purchase a self-hypnosis tape designed to help listeners touch their past lives. One day when she entered her trance state while playing the tape, Jill visualized herself standing in a hilly countryside covered by tall grass. To her left were a man and a woman locked in an embrace. It seemed that they were afraid of being caught together. The name *Emily Brontë* came to Jill just before she departed her trance.

She then conceived a story in which Emily Brontë was not the lonely spinster of popular belief but rather had a forbidden Gypsy lover, who became the model for Heathcliff in *Wuthering Heights*.

"Do I think I was Emily Brontë in a former life?" Jill says. "No, I don't, but it was fun to try to jump into her skin."

"How much of a leap was it?" I ask.

"I don't know how I wrote that, but I didn't change a word of it, and my editor didn't change a word of it. And I ran it by some of the people that I met in the Brontë Society, who are nuts about the Brontës. They know every little detail. In the diary part of the manuscript, I made mention of a hawk that Emily had rescued on the moors, and I made it at a date after which the hawk had died. Well, he got redlined, but that was the only change. And I felt like if that's the only thing they could find, then I did my homework. And they all loved the voice."

That book, *Emily's Secret*, won Jill a Maggie Award and launched her career. Since then have come ten more books in less than eight years.

"So you've been writing them at nearly a rate of three books every two years. Is that a matter of contractual deadline pressure, or do you set your own pace?" I ask.

"Well, I can pretty much set my own pace, but two things. You need to be out there at least once a year if you're in the mass-market arena, to keep your name in front of people. And to make some money. You know, one book a year is about the minimum for genre fiction. Now, if you're writing the Great American Novel, people can take ten years to do it, I suppose. But if you're writing romance or mystery or suspense or Westerns or sci-fi/fantasy—the paperback market—you've got to keep something out there about once a year or more."

Given that pressure to maintain a presence in the marketplace, competition for space in bookstores is stiff. Genre fiction has a high turnover rate and therefore a small window in which to grab a readership; romance novels, mysteries, and Westerns are pulled from shelves quicker than, say, psychology titles and history books. It's a testament to the popularity of genre novels that they can sell three or four times—first in retail bookstores and then repeatedly in secondhand paperback shops and at flea markets. In fact, if you want to peruse the full set of titles by Jill Jones or anyone else who isn't a top-ten name in their genre, the best place to do so is an aftermarket store.

I hesitate to share this with Jill, not knowing how she'd react, but my own copies of her novels came from a secondhand outlet. My *Essence of My Desire* bears the initials of a previous owner—*GB* or *GR*, I can't tell for sure which.

But I am bold enough to inquire about her attitude toward such outlets: "How do you feel about aftermarket stores? Are you glad to have the readers, or do you resent that you get no royalties on all the copies that are resold?"

"I think that they are very helpful to people like me who are not exactly brand names, because it gives readers a way to try my work. The people who go to those kind of stores are avid readers. Oftentimes, they'll pick up a new author, and they'll find they like that author, and they'll go and buy all their books. So, to me, it's an advertising thing. Some of the people who read romance read five or six books a week. They're just amazing! And they'll buy new books, and they'll buy used books—they'll do both."

Toward the end of our conversation, I make an error of definition when I try to trace Jill's career. "You started out with three historical novels, then went to mainstream romance. Lately, it seems you've gone to gothics. Are you just trying out different styles?"

"Now, I do not write historical novels. None of my books are historical. They are about contemporary people that get involved with a secret from the past, whether the secret's about Emily Brontë or a magical perfume.

"But you've hit my Achilles heel, and I'll tell you why. If you're a genre writer, you really need to be consistent in doing kind of the same thing over and over and over. And I did, the first three. But one thing kind of morphed into another, and it was a mistake for me to do that, because after nine books, I had gone from romance with a historical aspect to suspense novels. And that's where I really would like to be. I never did see myself as a romance writer so much, because I like romantic suspense.

"Pocket Books has just asked me to write straight suspense now, so I'm pretty happy about that. It's still genre, it's still commercial fiction, but I'd rather be a suspense writer than a romance writer. It took me nine books to figure that out."

"We had our honeymoon out here, the bride and I. And then we were coming two or three times a year, and eventually spending weeks at a time."

Randy Russell is telling me how he came to settle in the North Carolina mountains.

"I find it's the perfect place to . . . I hesitate to say 'be a writer,' because that's kind of limiting. But it's a community where it's pretty well accepted that many people are interested in things other than their day jobs.

"My wife and I had a fellow put roofs on the front and back of our house so we could build decks under them. I work at home, so I was here when they were working. One day, I went out, and they're both on the roof, about to finish it, and the fellow in charge turned to me and said, 'Randy, you know, I'm really an artist. I'm not a carpenter.'

"In Asheville, that's normal. That's more than normal. It's what just about everyone will tell you."

I know Randy from editing a couple of folklore collections he put together for my company. But I'm more interested in what he did before he came to us—the series of genre mysteries he wrote for Bantam/Doubleday around 1990. I want to know how he got his shot at the big time, and why he ultimately fell out of the running.

"I started out in poetry. While I was still in school, I had the *Paris Review* take two poems. It was the highlight of my life, and I got thirty-five dollars. At one point, I just sat down as I was getting out of school and started thinking, 'I've got to learn what book-length writing is,' and that's when I decided to write a mystery, because that was something I enjoyed reading.

"My editor at Bantam, when he saw my first manuscript, rejected it based on three or four problems. And I addressed those and sent it back to him, and he took the manuscript. Now, I think part of that was my willingness to follow his suggestions. I think he honestly believed in and improved the book.

"The first Rooster Franklin mystery was first person, and my editor said, 'This is fun. This is an interesting character, but it's not a series character.' So for the second book, I wrote an entirely different character, another set of circumstances. It was still set in Kansas City, and I wrote it in third person. As that was going through production, the first book got a really nice review in the *New York Times*, and they reprinted it, and it got an Edgar nomination. And so the publisher decided suddenly that the only thing that anyone would be interested in reading was the same character again.

"Now, I'd completed this book and turned it in and been paid for it, and I got the phone call: 'We want you to change this to Rooster Franklin and take it back to first person and make it your second Rooster Franklin book.' And being a cocky kid, I said no. So they let me keep the advance and killed the contract on that book. But at the same time, I'd been working on a third one, and I sent that in, and I got a contract for two more. So my third one actually became my second one, and the one they had rejected I went ahead and switched back to Rooster Franklin. They bought it, but they had to buy it again.

"To tell you the truth, to have a fiction manuscript accepted—I'm sure you might sympathize with this—and have them say, 'Change the main character, and change it from third to first person,' to me was writing a whole new book, so that's mainly why I said no.

"Steve, these people don't care about ten, fifteen thousand dollars. Do you know what I mean? At the time, I thought, 'Boy, I'm something. I taught them a lesson.' But it's not anything they probably spent more than ten minutes thinking about. It's funny."

Randy knows about *funny*. He's a big man with a big, rich laugh that he employs frequently. His mystery hero—Alton Benjamin "Rooster" Franklin, GED—bears the name of one of his best real-life friends, though that friend doesn't share the fictional Rooster's penchant for car boosting, gun play, and womanizing. Other friends appear, dressed and undressed, under their actual names, too. But being Randy's buddies, they don't particularly mind.

"To Steve, another obscure title for your home!" reads the inscription on my copy of one of his mysteries.

My favorite Randy Russell story involves the time he was mistakenly booked as a dog psychologist on a live, hour-long radio call-in program in Kansas City. Not learning of the error until he was on the air, he decided to fulfill his obligation, figuring that dog psychology isn't much different from human psychology—another subject he admits to knowing little about.

"Either your roommate or your dog must go," he advised one caller. "And we both know dogs are unable to pay rent elsewhere. Besides, your roommate doesn't jump on your bed and lick your face in the morning, does he?"

He told an attorney to get on all fours to commiserate with his cocker spaniel. "Try wiggling your rear end a little bit. That's a sign of confidence among dogs. And don't be afraid to show your teeth."

One caller expressed concern that her dog was afraid of birds.

"He should be," Randy opined. "Didn't you see that Hitchcock movie? Lots of dogs did."

A woman complained that her dog had a habit of drinking from the toilet. "My husband never puts the lid down," she said.

"What lid?"

One caller wanted to know how to stop her dog's barking.

"Dogs respond to positive rewards much more effectively than they respond to punishment. Whenever your dog isn't barking, give him a cookie."

Randy didn't get a return engagement.

"Why did you stop writing mysteries?" I ask him. "Too much deadline pressure?"

"No, they didn't sell well enough. My editor went to take over the Book-of-the-Month Club, and I got tossed to another editor. But it was mainly just because there wasn't money for the publisher. Four books is a pretty good test run, and it didn't climb the ladder. When my editor left, there was nobody left to support me, nobody in the accounting department who was going to show up at the board meeting and say, 'Keep publishing the guy.' And that's commercial fiction. That's a whole different approach from an editor who is grooming a major literary talent, and they know they're not going to make a lot of money off of them. But when you do commercial mysteries, they sink or swim, and most of them sink, financially, for the publishers.

"That's part of it. The whole trend in mysteries at that time was, though I hate to use the phrase, the *female sleuth*. Romance writers were moving over to mysteries and finding success, and all these little mystery bookstores were opening up, which generally were catering to women. People started finding out that women bought most of the books.

"The reason I can't say hard-boiled hit a wall is because the top guys kept selling. I mean, Elmore Leonard doesn't have any problems."

"So that was the end of the line?" I ask.

"I had an offer to do a police procedural—a bunch-of-cops type of story. I started to work on that, and I had no interest in it whatsoever. And of course, I was thinking I could do something else that I was more inclined to do and sell that instead of doing what they'd asked me to do. And I kind of quickly learned that when publishers ask you for something, your best bet is to go with it, if you want to continue to publish with them."

Now, Randy writes what he likes to write, and at a pace of his own choosing.

"I was thinking when I turned fifty, I'd write another mystery novel—I mean, a basic crime story. I do still consider myself a writer. I live a writer's life of the mind. I live a life of my own mythology, which I probably spend more time creating and honing than I do anything I've written or will write. The environment here and the people both contribute to that. I find it easy here. But I don't think I'll return to mysteries. Lots of people I've met have made very good livings doing it, and a lot of friends starved doing it."

His day job, such as it is, involves researching Southern antiquities and attending estate sales and auctions. He acquires personal artifacts and then sells them through direct contacts or via the Internet.

"That's where I concentrate in my historical antiques— my life that actually makes money. Prominence is about the only thing I care about. Southern estates, basically. There's rewards for research into these area, let me put it that way.

"Any antique that's a hundred years old, if it's just sitting on a shelf, has a certain value. But if you can learn who owned it and where they lived, and then perhaps find a photo in their photo album of them with that object, it's worth three times as much.

"And part of it is that stories become attached to artifacts, and I think people enjoy that. I know I do. When I sell something, I think I'm selling a story. And so that's what I do when I go to estate sales and hang out at auctions. I'm actually in some sense robbing the dead, because a lot of that stuff comes to auction when people pass away. I do collect people's lives that way. You know, there's a couple of university collections here in North Carolina that have benefited from my efforts.

"When I go to the barbershop and the barber says, 'What do you do for a living?' it's like I can't think of a thing to tell him. And the only answer I've come up with, which I have not had the courage yet to speak to a stranger, is to say, 'I collect people's lives.'"

I have doubts about contacting Bill Brooks. Has he heard about the writers' group tiff? Is it right for me to turn around and ask him for help now?

Since I wrote about him in the writers' group minutes, I've met Bill at an autographing and had him sign one of his books for me. He's also submitted a portion of a novel to my company. We rejected it, but no ill feelings ensued. In fact, he wrote us a classy note thanking us for our time.

I feel my manuscript would profit from another genre writer's input, and I'd be a coward not to pursue Bill: that's what finally decides the issue. He can tell me to kiss off if he wants.

When I finally get hold of him, he couldn't be more accommodating.

"You're up to, what, eleven titles now?" I ask him.

"Well, I have ten published, and I have five more that'll be coming out in the next nine months," he tells me.

Bill came to the area from Arizona. His father's family's roots are in Knoxville in eastern Tennessee, so moving to Asheville "was kind of like coming home for me." In Arizona, Bill worked as a guide, taking tourists into the mountains in a Jeep. His principal career before taking up teaching and writing was in health care. He began as a respiratory therapist and later set up cardiopulmonary departments in hospitals. "Before that, I had done all kinds of jobs—shoe sales, shipyards. Typical writer's background.

"From the time I was a kid, I always had a vast interest in Western culture. Of course, back in those days, there were a lot of cowboy movies. I found the history of the West from about 1800 to the late 1800s to be pretty fascinating because of all the famous and infamous characters of that period.

"When I decided to become a writer back in eighty-nine, I had no idea. They always say, 'Write what you know,' and at that point, I didn't think I knew hardly anything worth writing about. And I did a little research and found out that genre writing was still the easiest way to get published. And then it dawned on me that I did know something, and that was American history. So I thought, 'Well, I'll write a Western.' And I did that, and actually sold it to the second publisher I sent it to."

Bill's first nine books were genre shoot-'em-ups, after which he decided to make the leap to mainstream literary fiction with a Western bent.

"I was just getting tired of writing that stuff. And I'd always been fascinated by Billy the Kid. I did a little research and found out more books were written on Billy the Kid than on George Washington. So I knew that if I was going to take on that subject, I had to have something unique. And the mystery of Pat Garrett's death was a real hook for the editor."

Pat Garrett was the sheriff who ambushed Billy the Kid

in 1881. But since the killing took place in a darkened cabin, and since the speedy burial prevented a careful identification, it has long been speculated that someone other than Billy was the victim that night.

Bill Brooks took that circumstance and the unsolved murder of Pat Garrett in 1908 as his jumping-off points. What if there was a tacit understanding between Billy and Garrett that Billy would move away and live under a different name and Garrett would take credit for his killing? What if Billy spent nearly three decades quietly plotting Garrett's murder?

The book was called *The Stone Garden*.

"Brooks' novel deserves to be mentioned with such western classics as *Shane, Hombre*, and *The Virginian*," according to *Booklist*. "This is one of the most inventive, moving, and memorable western novels in many years." *Publishers Weekly* said that "this well-crafted tale is a graceful song, alive with drama, biting wit and just enough well-substantiated doubt to make you wonder."

"I wanted it to be lyrical," Bill tells me. "There are poetic passages throughout the thing. I knew I was taking a huge risk that no publisher would buy it. But they were intrigued by that mystery, so they went ahead and bought it, and I felt that I had latched onto a niche, which was to write these sort of lyrical fictional memoirs of true people."

After *The Stone Garden* come treatments of Pretty Boy Floyd and Bonnie and Clyde—two of the five books Bill has in the pipeline at the time I speak with him.

"And then you're going back to genre Westerns?" I ask.

"I just finished a deal with HarperCollins for a new

Western series called *Law for Hire*. We came up with the idea that the character would be a Pinkerton agent, and that he'd end up guarding famous people like Hickok and Cody and Masterson. The deal is, if I can write three books in nine months, I'll get all my money in nine months. I really see it as sort of a personal challenge, even though I don't want to write any more Westerns. If I'm a true working writer, can I do that?"

I'm flummoxed. "That's a rate of about . . . Say ninety days per book, that's a rate of about four published pages per day."

"Something like that. It'll probably end up more than that because I actually threw away the first hundred and some pages. It just wasn't going right. That's not unusual for me. Once I get going, I usually write a chapter a day on that stuff. I consider them just money books, I guess. You know, not your pride-and-joy type of books like the Bonnie and Clyde and the Pretty Boy and *The Stone Garden*."

They may not be particularly dear to his heart, but Bill's Westerns are the best pure fun of the genre novels I've read. Kung Chow, toadying Chinese laundryman; Jonas Fly, snake-oil salesman and certified phrenologist; Valdalia Rose, tallest whore west of the Mississippi; Persimmon Bill Edwards, hard-luck rummy—the stock characters are welcome old friends. Badass hero Quint McCannon tracks down killers, eats hardtack and beef jerky, sleeps under the stars, gets double-crossed, and rubs elbows with John Wesley Hardin, Roy Bean, and George Custer as he quietly goes about his deadly business. My dog-eared copy of *Dust on the Wind*—purchased from the same secondhand shop where I bought

Jill Jones's romances, and bearing the marks of previous owners *ERL* and *BF*—shows evidence of having been well loved.

"I guess in your teaching, you've probably encountered a broad spectrum of people, from the talented to the pretty much hopeless," I say. "How far do you think writing can be taught? Is it mainly getting them to recognize their mistakes quicker than they would have on their own?"

"I think if you take a good writing course, you can cut your learning curve. As I try to tell everyone I work with, writing really is a craft, and you can teach craft. You can't teach talent, and you can't teach drive. But you can teach the craft of writing—protagonists, plot, dialogue, and all that sort of thing.

"What I find holds most of them back, if they have any sort of talent, is they lack drive. I would take somebody with a little less talent and a lot of drive and give them a better opportunity of getting published than somebody with a lot of talent and no drive.

"And what I quite often find in teaching adult students is a lot of them are working jobs, or they're married and living sort of moderately comfortable lives, and I think that just doesn't bode well for drive. I think you have to be hungry.

"So I've taught a lot of writers that I thought had wonderful talent, but I could just tell that they didn't work at it every day. They'd work only on inspiration, and whenever they got around to it. And I just knew that some of them weren't going to make it. I'd tell them, 'You can't make it on talent alone. You have to be driven and do this just like a job.'"

"Do you have any insights into what compels so many people to give it a try, even against a very poor likelihood of success?" I ask.

"It's not like when you see a beautiful painting and you decide, 'Well, I'm just going to go home and be another Raphael.' Because you'd have to learn all the skills—which brushes to use and colors to mix. But you're taught technically how to write at a very young age. You can find someone that has a strong interest in reading, and at some point they think, 'Aha! I could write a book better than this.'

"And everyone has an interesting life they want to write about. I think it was Samuel Goldwyn who once said, 'The only people that should write their memoirs are the dead.' And I think they feel they can make that leap from being an avid reader and having an interesting life story to writing creatively.

"And then they fall into the chasm, of course, or the abyss of hell."

Jill Jones raises the same point when I ask her about the writer's urge.

"You know, a lot of people want to write their grandmother's memoirs, or a story based on what Granny did," she tells me. "And I think those people are the ones that aren't going to make it, because they can't divorce fiction from fact. Fiction has its rules—especially genre fiction—and facts usually don't fit the rules.

"I think if people want to write, if that's their passion, it's not my job to talk them out of it. I do tell them the truth about the industry, and that's very discouraging. I just tell them, 'When you get this book finished, if they turn you down again and again and again and again and again—and it happens to everybody that ever writes—you've got to be able to handle it.'

"And then you get published, and you think you're hot potatoes and you're on your way, and they buy one book and they don't buy two. This has happened to friends of mine. They think they've stepped over that line and they're in, but that's not the way it is either. Once you're in the business, it's hard to stay in the business.

"But why do people want to write?" she says. "Beats me. It's the hardest work I've ever done."

A complication enters *Essence of My Desire*.

Through an old diary, Nick Rutledge learns a family secret. Back in the 1840s, his ancestor John Rutledge fell in love with Mary Rose Hatcher, an English witch. To prevent their union, John was exiled to India, where he was introduced to the mysterious *mahja* plant in a monastery at the foot of the Himalayas. He sent *mahja* seeds back to Mary Rose, who planted them, nurtured the flowers that grew, made a perfume from them, and dispatched a batch to John. That perfume permitted them to meet as lovers in their dreams. Unfortunately, repeated use transported them to such an exalted spiritual realm that they ceased to exist in a physical sense. They simply vanished, never to be heard from again.

Thus, when Nick Rutledge and Simone Lefèvre partake of the perfume in the present day, they do so at peril of annihilation.

Their dream meetings are just a tease anyway. What I'm

really anticipating is the scene when Nick and Simone get together in the flesh.

Randy Russell's mysteries and Bill Brooks's Westerns have love scenes, too, but they're nothing like Jill Jones's. Rooster Franklin's path is littered with naked women. In *Blind Spot*, he steals the limousine in which President Kennedy was shot, opens the trunk, and finds a beautiful, comatose woman wearing only a pair of panties. The female inhabitants of Quint McCannon's frontier towns are lonely widows and gold-hearted bar girls. There's no lovemaking in these books; it's quick, old-fashioned, pants-around-the-ankles banging. Whether or not the characters are spiritually fulfilled is beside the point.

Still on the outs, Nick and Simone fail in their separate attempts to duplicate the mysterious perfume synthetically. Meanwhile, vile Frenchman Antoine Dupuis gets hold of a sample and becomes addicted to it. The quarry in his dream-world love chase is, of course, Simone. Repeated mentions of the Frenchman's small stature hammer home his unattractiveness. Nick Rutledge's oft-lauded broad shoulders are the leading indicator of his desirability.

Finally, Nick and Simone resolve to try to heal their old wounds. They meet for dinner at a fancy place called, incredibly, the In and Out Club. They dance; they kiss; she cries. Nick invites her home. Simone declines but then follows him in a taxi to his London suburb for a night of passion.

A metaphorical sword is drawn.

Petals are parted.

On her departure the next morning, Simone steals Nick's vial of perfume. Later, racked by guilt, she barricades herself in an apartment and douses herself in the dangerous mixture, figuring the only way she can have Nick now is by crossing into the dream world permanently.

But Nick finds her, takes a splash of perfume himself, and journeys to the other realm to convince Simone of his love and bring her back.

Indeed, it is the love-addled Dupuis who overdoses and is dematerialized!

My glasses are fogged and my face a bit flushed as I turn the final page.

CHAPTER 9

Son of Bullitt

I drive like Mr. Magoo. I don't have an old-timey open-air car with a squeeze-ball horn, but I do share his near-sightedness, poor judgment, and easy confusion. I'm therefore a danger when I'm anxious and in a hurry, as now.

Going to my car one morning, I discover that its left rear tire is flat. I can't get a good look at the offending object, which protrudes a quarter-inch from the tire and splays like some jagged metal flower. On my knees in the drive-way, I touch it gingerly.

These days, I drive an aged white Olds, a model that was discontinued from production some years ago. I jack the back end but find that my tire wrench doesn't have a great-enough breadth to give me leverage to loosen the thor-oughly rusted bolts—just the kind of irregularity that sounded the car model's death knell, a wrench meant for a little red wagon.

I keep an aerosol tire inflater in the trunk. The way the white foam sputters from the puncture confirms my opinion that the wound is mortal.

I don't have time for this. I'm nervous and want to get to the office early.

My wife is on the phone in the kitchen, a vantage point from which she's witnessed my exertions over the tire—and no doubt narrated them to whoever it is she's talking to. I motion for her attention and explain how I'll have to stop at a service station to get the tire changed on the way to work.

"Don't be silly," she says. "Anyone can change a tire. I've done it myself."

I cup my hand to my ear, point to the telephone, plead for discretion.

The tires on the car when I bought it were a size that has since been eliminated from manufacturers' lines. The car has front-wheel drive, and the rear tires have worn so well that I continue to use my original set, though I've replaced the front pair. The car rides on tires of two different heights, then, but it's the larger size that I keep as a mounted spare. I've retained a smaller spare in case I blow a rear tire, but I don't have a rim for it.

I explain all of this to the mechanic with the aid of a couple of hand gestures—one that mimes the turning of a spigot and the other the plucking of grapes from a vine. I don't want the mounted spare on the back of the car. I want my backup, smaller-sized spare mounted on the damaged tire's rim.

The mechanic is an old, bearded cowboy who listens with his arms folded across his chest, moving his toothpick from one side of his mouth to the other with every few taps of his boot. He stoops over the tire, produces a pair of pliers from an unknown location on his person, and extracts the object, which proves to be a common nail with its head bent and split.

He turns on me accusatorially, with the terse contempt such men reserve for people who carry two spare tires. "Nothing wrong with this tire," he says.

I start to justify myself, but the mechanic swaggers into the other bay before I have a chance to formulate a clear position. I notice he doesn't even think enough of my nail to dispose of it properly, casually flicking it out the open door and into the lot, presumably to stick in someone else's tire. He returns with a tire-plugging kit, effects his repair, and inflates the tire. He then wipes his hands on a loathsome rag and runs the blade of his pocketknife under his fingernails while I fumble for my wallet.

I lay rubber as I exit the station.

I've set myself a firm goal. I can't continue investing time, travel, and money in my manuscript indefinitely. When I reach a certain page count—considerably less than the entire projected length—I'll quit work on it until I can find whether it might be worthy of publication. If the answer is yes, I'll continue to completion. If it is no, I'll scrap it for good. Of course, I'd be in a better position if I had a completed manuscript to offer, but I believe I've written enough for a fair judgment.

It is time, as my father used to say, to shit or get off the pot.

First, I show it to my boss at work and ask her advice on how I ought to proceed. She is aware of my general subject matter and has provided me some Asheville leads, but I've been tight-lipped about the personal nature of what I'm doing; she probably thinks I'm attempting a history of mountain writers. She's not fond of delivering hard news but doesn't shy from it either, so I'm confident her evaluation will be no kinder than what I deserve.

I give it to her on a Thursday or Friday and get it back first thing Monday morning.

"I started reading your manuscript and couldn't put it down," she says in her written evaluation. "Your self-deprecation made me laugh out loud at points." And later, "I know I'd be proud to publish this manuscript, but I think you might be doing yourself a disservice if you don't try to get a house that is better known for its literary publishing."

She goes on to discuss in some detail one chapter in which the narrative voice isn't of a kind with the rest of the manuscript. This last point notwithstanding, her words are balm. Her offer to publish is deeply appreciated, but it is my dream to land with a major house, as she understands.

Fixing the problem she identified requires me to switch the order of two chapters and completely rework one of them, cutting six to eight pages of material and writing four of five pages of new. But I don't lack for incentive. A week's worth of late nights finish the job. I then show the manuscript to another coworker, who makes no mention of any inconsistency of narrative voice and who is, to my delight, even more complimentary in his evaluation than our boss.

I am thus ready to brave the wider waters.

One of our company's best recent successes was a risky first novel that bounced around New York before making its way to us. It sold modestly in hardcover for us but garnered superior reviews. Soon, our author had himself a major paperback contract and deals for translations into several languages. When the paperback came out, it got glowing notice in the *New York Times Book Review*, a nearly unheard-of coup for a reprint edition. By then, the author had a second manuscript, to which we held the right of first refusal. Of course, he'd priced himself out of our market by then, but we made a token offer so as to give him and his agent a floor from which to proceed. The author shortly won a two-book deal with a mega-house. It was an amicable parting. We were pleased to bask in his success, and he was grateful for the path we'd provided him.

I don't claim credit for any of this. The manuscript required some cleaning up, but by and large, it had come to us much as we published it. Before it was ever accepted, however, I recognized its merits and argued its case when not everyone on our staff was in agreement.

The upshot for me is that I have an easy entrée to a young agent on the rise. It is partly thanks to me that he now boasts a talented, ambitious author ripe for big things. Perhaps my name has been mentioned during the behind-the-scenes doings. If not, the agent still might be kindly disposed when I come forward with a manuscript of my own.

I ask my boss to run interference for me.

I don't know exactly what she writes the agent, beyond telling him of my years with the company and praising my manuscript and my writing and editing generally. But I am privy to the agent's reply to her. In three dashed-off but nonetheless memorable lines, he declares himself both "thrilled" and "delighted" at the prospect of seeing my work, refers to me familiarly as "Steve K.," and vows to read my stuff as quickly as he can upon its arrival.

Of course, I want to get the manuscript into his hands before his enthusiasm has a chance to wane. I spend a couple of fretful days in writing, rewriting, and re-rewriting a cover letter. The letter has to provide my contact information, establish my connection to the agent via our mutual author, describe my industry experience and editing credits, highlight my previous publications, and, most importantly, summarize, capture the essence of, and make irresistible the material I am presenting to him. And it has to do all this without a bragging tone in one artful single-spaced page.

Since I am providing him only half the manuscript I project, I synopsize the remainder of the book, promising insight, historical perspective, more than a little poignancy, and much hilarity.

When I'm ready to send my package, I don't leave it with the outgoing office mail but take it straight to the post office, where I don't drop it in an outside box or even slip it through the slot inside the building but deliver it directly to the care of the overfed man behind the counter.

I don't maneuver through traffic as much as I avoid objects hurtling toward my stationary position, as in an arcade game. My vision narrows to the hundred yards of pavement directly in front of me. My mind is drawn to irrelevancies. People riding with me make frequent use of their imaginary brake pedal. Other motorists give me room.

My route lies along the heavily trafficked interstate that bisects town. I settle in behind a pickup pulling a trailer loaded with lawn equipment. The driver stretches to fumble in the glove compartment, and I remark something familiar in my glimpse of his profile. Mr. Epps? I nudge the gas pedal and move closer. One of my daughters took science from Epps—a man with sour breath and a pocketful of mechanical pencils, as I recall from open-house night. Things aren't so dire that teachers have to spend the summer mowing grass, are they?

I'm getting too close. He taps his brakes to back me off.

Suddenly, Epps—or whoever he is—exits right. The traffic in the left lane disperses. I hear the whoosh of air brakes behind me and take a glance in the mirror to discover a big truck shockingly tight on my bumper. It seems to be angry about something.

Going uphill now, the truck fades until it's a blister on the mirror and the sounds of its downshifting are as subtle as pangs of conscience. Downhill, it swings into the passing lane and closes the distance with frightening speed. It draws abreast at the bottom of the hill. For one brief moment, I look up into the face of the copilot—scornful, sunglassed, street-smart. The truck gains ground at a decreased rate. My car is opposite the middle of the trailer as the next hill steepens. Then the truck again falls behind me and moves back into the right-hand lane.

Downhill this time, the passing lane is repopulated by motorists comfortable in their knowledge that the beast has singled out its prey. The truck can't swing wide. It stays tight on my bumper, its air brakes whooshing every few seconds. Unaccountably, I back off the throttle. The speedometer dips from fifty-three to fifty to forty-five and levels out at forty-two. The trucker lays into his air horn so long and loud that my head sinks protectively between my shoulders and the hair on my neck stands smartly. The truck has fallen back enough now that I can see they're flipping me the bird—both of them, with both hands each.

An exit ramp miraculously presents itself, and I throttle up and swing hard right. The truck hurtles past, its horn still blaring but mellowing like that of a train entering a tunnel.

For time immemorial, the central moment of the day for writers has been the arrival of the postman.

My wife gets home from work earlier than I do, so my habit is to call every afternoon beginning a week after I posted my manuscript. I understand that this is premature, as my package could hardly have gone to New York and been routed directly back in that length of time. Still, I have to inquire. In fact, I have my wife's homecomings so well timed that I usually catch her coming in the door, so she has to run for the phone to keep the answering machine from picking up. She's slightly breathless when she answers—irked, too.

"Anything come today?"

"Just bills and junk."

Or "Did you get the mail on the way in?"

"I just dropped it on the kitchen table."

"And?"

"I didn't see what you're looking for."

Of course, I'm not looking for my return envelope back, as that would indicate a bad outcome. What I'm really expecting is a phone call at work. Even if the agent doesn't want to handle my manuscript, I suspect my writing is good enough and that I've banked sufficient industry coin to merit at least a courtesy conversation.

But I receive no word by mail or phone.

At work, I'm editing a book about the Trail of Tears of 1838, during which tens of thousands of Cherokees living mainly in Georgia, North Carolina, Tennessee, and Alabama were compelled to give up their homelands and undertake forced migrations to the West. United States soldiers under General Winfield Scott took to the countryside with rifles and bayonets, rounding up men in the fields, women in their homes, and children at play. They drove the Cherokees to stockades, where they were warehoused until enough of them could be gathered to comprise a "detachment" to Oklahoma, some twenty-two of which were organized in all. A great number of Cherokees died during the journey west, and many of those who made it to their unwanted new home arrived bereaved and hopeless.

Actually, I'm editing the editor, as the book is a compilation of firsthand accounts of the migration, for which the editor has provided a preface, a lengthy introduction, brief lead-ins to the various excerpts of source material, and all the necessary documentation.

Within two weeks, I finish the preface, the introduction, and most of the main text. Within a month, I complete most of the grunt work—bibliography, endnotes, and such—which leaves me only to write the jacket copy and polish off some miscellaneous small tasks. Within six weeks, I am well into editing the next book in line, a guide to romantic sites in the Southeast.

It's my observation that if deals in the industry are going to be struck, things tend to progress quickly. If I haven't heard by now, then the news is bad.

I don't know that I've ever suffered what would qualify as depression, but I'm certainly not sowing much joy these days. At work, I'm less prone to idle talk; I stick to my office and actually get more done than usual. At home, I cease caring whether the kids pick up their stuff or do their homework; I am less inclined to anger but also immune to laughter. Blanketing everything is numbness and a feeling of worthlessness—or foolishness, maybe, for having squandered so much time, energy, and hope. I look forward all day to going to bed. I understand how weak and self-pitying I'm being.

Within two months, I am on the verge of finishing the romantic guide.

At ten weeks, I finally contact the agent by e-mail: "Did you receive a manuscript from me around May 1?"

I have a reply within the hour: No, he did not.

I don't doubt his truthfulness. Publishers and agents receive thousands of submissions per year, and some parcels are lost. More likely, a staffer opened my manuscript, didn't care much for it, and discarded it, not knowing the agent had agreed to review it himself.

Having committed myself to seeing the process through,

I change the date on my cover letter and send another copy of the manuscript, this time via one of the overnight carriers. But it is a foregone conclusion what will happen now. It's an unspoken rule in the business not to establish yourself as a pain in the ass by bugging people, even for so legitimate a reason as inquiring about your lost package. I'll get a prompt reply the second time around, and it will certainly be a rejection.

I e-mail the agent two weeks after sending my package to make sure he's gotten it.

Indeed he has, he e-mails me back. He says he has a considerable backlog of manuscripts but will get to mine as soon as he can.

Four days after that, the package is in my mailbox. My wife doesn't tell me but lets me find it when I get home. I've stopped calling and asking by then.

The agent begins by saying that, in his experience, editors aren't fond of narrative nonfiction by struggling writers who make getting published a central issue in their manuscripts. But even given the unpopularity of my subject matter, he'd take me on as a client if he found my writing engaging enough. Sadly, he didn't. He closes by recommending that I try small publishers, as he feels I might have a large niche market among the kind of fellow wannabes who fill the seats at writers' conferences.

I can't really argue with any of this. His remarks on manuscripts about struggling writers aren't what I expected—in fact, I figured my subject might be of special interest to people in the trade—but his experience with big-city editors trumps my uninformed hopes. His indifference toward my writing is more damning. At the company where I work, people frequently call or write us after their manuscripts have been rejected. They tell us why their submissions should have been accepted; they question our judgment; they demand detailed critiques, with which they then take issue in further communications. But it's all pretty simple. Your stuff either works or it doesn't. I've never known editors to come to like a rejected manuscript because an author persuades them of its merit.

Having no cause for complaint, I drop the agent a line thanking him for his consideration.

One benefit of my long wait is that I'd had plenty of time to lay contingency plans. My second choice is an agent with whom I've enjoyed a telephone acquaintance for a couple of years. I edited a novel by a rather difficult author of hers, who spoke kindly of my efforts to the agent, at no bidding by me. Now, I contact the agent to ask if she'll consider representing me. She says she will, the only twist being that she wants to see not only my manuscript but the reviews of my first book as well. I have to go digging for the box where my clippings are yellowing. I try to remember if I might have overrepresented my success to the agent at some point. If so, it will come home to roost now. I have a couple of national reviews to offer, but most of it is local stuff.

My package goes out in early August. I figure I won't hear anything until after Labor Day, but I have it back a week before the holiday. The agent says she found my manuscript "hilarious and charming." But since I have no celebrity status—which, she admits, is opposite my purpose—she doubts she would be able to place my work. She feels I've also set myself a marketing challenge by focusing on the difficulties of the writer's life, since my potential audience figures to be more inclined toward messages of hope and inspiration.

I have in mind a couple other agents, then four or five editors to whom I might submit directly. But it's dawning on me—just as I learned years ago sending out short stories—that I don't have the temperament to wait through ten or twenty or thirty or forty rejections. My material would be so dated by that point that there'd be no point in picking it back up. And I can't see myself submitting to dozens of places simultaneously, like everyone else does. Receiving all those rejections en masse would play hell with me.

Spending years on a manuscript and then quitting after only two submissions has to constitute a record for raising the white flag, I know. Lately, however, I've been considering a couple other projects that would be easier, less personally embarrassing, and more likely to find a home—though they'd also hold no possibility of being special.

To help me decide, I approach my coworkers individually and ask them for a reading.

I pull into the parking lot at a nail salon, where I get out and drop to one knee to check my bad tire.

From my ground-level perspective, the car's defects reveal themselves one by one—the copious rust in the wheel well, the loose molding along the top of the back window where rain seeps in, the long scratch where I sideswiped a dumpster. With the taller tires in front and the car's natural posture of squatting on its haunches, it gives the impression that it's traveling perpetually uphill. The new plug, which stuck from the tire like a worm from an apple when the mechanic installed it, now has the texture of gum with road pebbles embedded in it. A little of the tire inflater's latex, which has by now deteriorated to a viscous white liquid, still percolates around the puncture.

I've left the interstate a couple of exits early, and there doesn't seem to be an entrance ramp at this location. I find myself in an unfamiliar hard-luck neighborhood where broken glass glitters in the streets and toddlers run naked in the yards. Asking directions seems like a bad idea.

I select the likeliest-looking route as each choice presents itself, yet my course deteriorates from four lanes to two lanes with markings to an unmarked lane and a half of two-way traffic with illegal parking on both sides of the street.

Half a block ahead, a battered sedan backs out of a driveway and stalls with its trunk protruding beyond the row of parked cars. I slow to let it in ahead of me, but it stalls twice more, so I toot my horn and squeeze past. I'm running late, and I don't know exactly where I am.

A cat darts under my wheels at the same moment a bucket of water hits the side of my car. The cat escapes beyond the vehicles on the right while its tormentor, an obese woman in stretch pants, swears hotly from the left. My window is cracked, so I idle along while feeling under the seat for something to use to dry myself. In the mirror, I see the sedan emerging from a cloud of blue smoke some distance behind.

It catches me within a couple of blocks, follows me for another, and then pulls out to pass, only to begin misfiring on one of its cylinders when it's abreast of my rear bumper. There's no room to pass anyway. A car approaches head-on, and the sedan falls in behind me.

The next time I glance in the mirror, I see the driver motioning me off the road. I try to oblige, easing in between two parked cars, but the sedan has slowed, too, the driver ripping a packet of sugar with his teeth and adding it to a cup of coffee balanced precariously on the dashboard.

My magnanimity spurned, I reenter traffic. The sedan's driver motions me off the road again. I tap my brake and make as if to pull aside, then accelerate smartly when the sedan starts to swing around me. To hell with him. I'm in as much of a hurry as he is.

I continue straight at the next intersection, but the sedan turns right and greases the pavement in accelerating. I look right at the next two intersections in vain. By the third, the sedan has pulled even with me a block over, and there's a fraction of a second when the driver's eyes hatefully challenge my own.

The sedan must come upon some difficulty in the next block, as it's a full car length behind me at the fourth intersection. It then assumes the lead and is out of sight for the next two blocks, its blue smoke the only witness to its passing.

I glance right at the following corner and nearly foul myself when I see it bearing down on me from the perpendicular at a distance of thirty or forty feet. It turns and fishtails in behind, the driver pounding the dashboard in frustration. The coffee is nowhere to be seen; it's probably in his lap, which would help account for his mood. I'm pleased that I'm still in the lead, though I find it hard to believe that the route we're traveling leads anywhere of importance.

That judgment proves premature when the street straightens and widens and a smattering of marginal businesses rear their shaggy heads—a martial-arts academy, a laundromat, a fish market.

I know the way to work now.

A narrow shoulder begins, and the sedan's driver motions me aside emphatically. When I fail to obey, he crosses the double yellow lines and pulls out to pass. The sedan is hitting on all cylinders now, but I punch the accelerator and maintain a slight lead through forty, forty-five, and fifty in a thirty-miles-per-hour zone.

No oncoming traffic is in sight. The sedan draws even crossing an overpass. The driver yells something through his open passenger window that's obscured by the bridge noise. I crank my window and angle my ear into the wind, trying to catch the insult. He's leaning as far toward me as he can, steering with his left hand.

I'm anticipating something I'd be hesitant to put in print. He's driving with two fingers now, yelling his lungs out. The coffee indeed shows on his shirt.

He digs deeply into some untapped vocal reserve. This time, the message is hoarse but clear: "If you can't drive, get off the road!"

The sentiment may be simple, but I have to admire how he's crystallized twenty-some years of bad driving under such a tidy umbrella.

The sedan accelerates past. I finally let it go.

In the parking lot at work, I sit for a minute listening to the metal tick as the car begins to cool. I catch a stale, sweet whiff of antifreeze.

The first of my coworkers to read my manuscript spent ten minutes in my office laughing with me over what he judged to be the funny parts.

Another employee shared her copy with two additional people barely known to me, who enjoyed it as much as she had.

A third read it and also gave it to her husband, who was so generous as to write me a critique.

There were suggestions and criticisms, to be sure. And I'm well aware of the perils of sharing a manuscript with one's friends.

But why look far afield?

It was my intention to beat my boss to the office this morning, but she's already talking with someone. I linger near her doorway until she's off the phone.

"Say, does that offer to publish my book still stand?"

CHAPTER 10

Girl Power

I have doubts about Father Tim Kavanagh, the hero of Jan Karon's Mitford novels.

Father Tim plants flowers. He likes to plan menus and host small dinner parties. He quotes scripture to calm his dog. He's all atwitter at the prospect of kissing a woman; he's sixty and virginal. He's flaccid and nurturing. He's cuddly; he'd make a good plush toy.

I try to think of a way to frame my opinion. "This guy Father Tim," I say to my wife, who's read all the books, "seems like sort of a pantywaist."

I mean that in the best sense of the word, but her look tells me I've missed the point again.

"Not at all," she says. "He's the ideal man."

If Father Tim is a woman in man's clothing, then it's

past time for some payback. Female readers have certainly suffered male authors' perspectives plenty long.

"I've talked to male writers who are feeling some pressure to try to address the female portion of their audience," I remark to Ann B. Ross, author of the Miss Julia novels.

"Right, but I wish they wouldn't do it," she says. "I'll tell you, the worst thing in the world to me is a male writer trying to write from a woman's viewpoint. Those characters are the most aggressively sexual. It's dream fulfillment, wish fulfillment, I think they're doing."

Anyone who's made even a casual observation can tell you that women buy most of the books sold. Women rival men on the bestseller lists. They're prominent among editors, agents, and reviewers. And their gentling influence has extended across the gender line. The prototype for a male author today is a family-man writing professor with a mortgage, not a dissolute cocksman in the mold of Wolfe or Fitzgerald.

Jan Karon was born Janice Meredith Wilson, named for the title character of the Paul Leicester Ford bestseller written partly at Biltmore House. It proved an uncanny choice. In the opening scene of *Janice Meredith*, the fifteen-year-old heroine is caught reading on the Sabbath. "Oh, mommy," Janice implores, "punish me as much as you please,—I know 't was very, very wicked,—but please don't take the book away!"

"Not another sight shalt thou have of it, miss," her mother replies. "My daughter reading novels, indeed!"

Karon grew up on a farm in the North Carolina foothills town of Lenoir. She completed her first novel at age ten and sought to keep it hidden from her sister, who of course found it and focused her entire critical attention on the single dirty word buried in the manuscript: *damn*. A lecture and whipping followed for Jan. She has kept it clean ever since.

Life intervened before she could pursue her dream of being a novelist. Karon doesn't like to reveal much about her private life, but it is known that her father left home when she was three and that her grandparents raised her. She quit school following the eighth grade. Before she was out of her teens, she had a daughter and a broken marriage.

At eighteen, she took a job as a receptionist at an advertising agency, where she kept leaving writing samples on her boss's desk until he promoted her. She fashioned a highly successful career, taking assignments in New York and San Francisco, winning industry awards, handling accounts like Honda and British Airways, and ultimately rising to the position of creative vice president with a national agency.

"I was called to be a writer," she said in a public-radio interview. "I didn't answer that call for many, many years. For one thing, I didn't know how to write a book. I had a daughter to raise. I waited until I was forty-eight. But I knew that if I didn't do something soon to act upon my calling, I'd be an old ad hack in the back room."

So she sold her big house with the beautiful gardens, gave up her health insurance, traded her Mercedes for a rusty Toyota, and moved to a cottage in the mountain resort village of Blowing Rock, an hour and a half north of Asheville on the Blue Ridge Parkway.

She started with a title and an outline. "It just didn't

work," she said. "The characters just didn't come together. Finally, in despair, I just gave up. I thought, I've done a foolish and impetuous thing, and everyone will laugh at me. Then, one night, when I was in bed, I had a simple mental image of a priest walking down a village street, and he went to a dog named Barnabas, and they went to a boy named Dooley."

She began writing about Father Tim and took some samples to Jerry Burns, the editor of the local weekly newspaper, the *Blowing Rocket*.

"Jan wanted to test the waters, to see if she could write, to see if people were interested in her kind of story—no sex, no violence, no language," Burns tells me.

She had a good concept. He, like all editors of small weeklies, had a need of material. He agreed to give her a chance.

Burns originally saw it as perhaps a three-month run, but subscriptions went up, and people kept asking when the next installment of "Father Tim—The Mitford Years" would be printed. He encouraged her to keep going. The series ultimately ran for a little over two years in the early 1990s.

It's easy to see that Blowing Rock was the model for friendly, comfortable Mitford. I've called Jerry Burns to ask if I can stop by the office and browse the original serial run, but my car overheats on the way up the mountain, so I don't arrive until eleven-thirty. Burns and the office manager—the only other person at the *Rocket*—have a lunch appointment at noon. Though he's never laid eyes on me before, Burns doesn't even hesitate: I'm welcome to stay alone in the office while they're away. What's more, he'll give me a key to the place. If I decide to leave, I should lock up behind me and drop the key through the slot.

The April 6, 1990, issue of the *Rocket* ran sixteen pages and sold for ten cents; the yearly subscription rate was ten dollars in North Carolina and twelve outside the state. There are two pictures on the front page. One is of the Penderecki String Quartet, "one of Poland's finest chamber ensembles," scheduled to perform at the Blowing Rock Arts Center ten days hence. The other shows the fledgling author holding her dog. "Jan Karon's 'Father Tim—The Mitford Years' begins this week," the caption says. "Scheduled to appear weekly in the *Blowing Rocket*, the feature will share the everyday trials and tribulations of Father Tim as he goes about his parish duties."

Inside the paper, an illustration by Jan's own hand decorates the first installment. It's Father Tim's face viewed straight on. He's bald save for a single tuft in the middle and a dark fringe around the sides. He wears round glasses and a preacher's collar. It's a prototype for the drawings that will later appear in more than eight million copies of Jan's books.

An editor's note promises that the columns "will give readers an opportunity to enjoy a return to the writing style and content of newspapers of a previous era, when fictional serials were the dominant theme of major newspapers around the world."

The principal difference between Jan's original serial and *At Home in Mitford*, the first of the novels, is that the opening several installments in the *Rocket* focus almost exclusively on Father Tim's adoption of Barnabas the dog. By the time she reworked the columns in novel form, Jan had the good sense to get her several story lines up and running earlier, which makes the novel version quicker and tighter. I don't have the time to compare the two side by side at length, but she seems to have found the rhythm that would carry through the entire novel series by the eighth or ninth column.

Of greater interest is the author's note that follows the farewell installment in the *Rocket* of April 24, 1992. After thanking her friends, neighbors, and readers, Jan promises "a long list of acknowledgments in the book when it's published.

"So, when is it going to be published?" she continues.

"The answer is:

"I don't know.

"Two well-known publishing houses have declined the manuscript, one 'after several careful readings.'

"Does this mean it's not a good book?

"Not necessarily.

"Agatha Christie sent her first novel off to five houses before she got an acceptance. Beatrix Potter, discouraged because no one wanted to publish Peter Rabbit, decided to self-publish. Ten years later, the little book was selling in the millions. . . .

"The good news is that I believe in this simple, wholesome book with its genuine, ordinary people. Now, all we have to do is find an editor with whom the chemistry is right. . . .

"If you'd like to see more wholesome fiction on shelves that are overcrowded with the lurid and sensational, please pray for Father Tim. . . .

"P.S. Several readers have written to say they'll miss Father Tim and all the gang. Actually, I've been missing them terribly since I completed the manuscript last October. So, I've decided to begin the sequel even before the original has found a publisher. This, my friends, is what's known as an act of faith."

Even when Karon located that special editor and publisher, her books weren't an instant success. My copy of *A Light in the Window*, the second Mitford novel, is a first edition—that is, a trade-paperback original bearing the imprint of Lion Publishing. Curious as to how the series found its first home with the now-defunct, Illinois-based subsidiary of a British house, I track down David Toht and Bob Klausmeier, her editors at Lion.

"I'm guessing she began like everyone else, trying the New York houses and not succeeding. Was that the case?" I ask Toht.

"Well, it's interesting," he says. "We kind of started the Mitford series because she *did* succeed with a New York house."

"Way back, the way we first got to know Jan was she sent us a children's book," Klausmeier says. "She originally sent it to the U.K., and the children's editor over there suggested she try through the American office. And so she sent me the children's picture book that became *Miss Fannie's Hat*. When we finally decided we wanted it, she had also sent it out to a New York house—Putnam, I believe—and they wanted it. And so she apologized and said, 'Well, I've got this serialized thing that I've been doing for the local paper, and it's actually a novel, or I'm planning to turn it into a novel. Would you like to look at that manuscript?' So I said sure, and she sent it on then, and that was the beginning, *At Home in Mitford*."

"We were very much impressed," Toht says. "Being a branch of an English company, we imported a lot of British books, with inevitably a British orientation. And these were so wonderfully American. I must say, I think we pretty early on thought that these were going to do well, certainly for us. Not as well as they finally did, but . . ."

"What was the arrangement?" I ask.

"We contracted for three books," Toht says. "They were just perfect for us. We were trying to produce books about orthodox Christianity without a distinct denominational relationship, books that would be of interest to people who were unfamiliar with the faith or outside the faith or also inside the faith—we called them 'gentle readers'—our assumption being that the Christian world view is one of many that can inform characters in a book, and be a perfectly valid approach. So we had fiction titles as well as general reference titles related to the Bible and the Christian faith, and a line of children's books."

"I guess the attractions of Jan's books were Father Tim himself, and the clean story, and the positive image of Christians," I say.

"In her books, aspects of the faith were really nicely integrated into the plot, because he's a priest. And they're also just great stories. I consider her really a humorist almost, because they're very, very entertaining books. But they weren't preachy books. That's what we were seeking, something that sort of integrated Christianity into good fiction."

"But the books didn't have much success with you, did they?"

"Five to ten thousand copies for the first year would have been fine," Toht says. "I cannot recall the numbers. We were in the turmoil of being sold. It was pretty nightmarish. The U.S. entity had never made a profit, so we were sold to David C. Cook. This was just about a year after we contracted with Jan. And that proved to be a pretty unsatisfactory marriage. Jan, among her many strengths, had really sound ideas for promoting her books, having been in advertising recently. Many of these she was going to handle herself at very low expense to the company. I was all for them, but the bosses just didn't agree that the books were worth promoting to the degree that they deserved.

"We knew we had something, but we didn't even get to the national book convention until after we were sold. And I remember, I really wanted to make the whole booth sort of a mini-Mitford, and just let that title be the one we really promoted, because we really felt good about it."

"How did things finally fall apart?" I ask.

"While I was there, we published the first one, and then I resigned and started my own business and was asked by the new Lion entity in the U.S. to edit her next two books. And then Jan called me and said she was really disappointed in how things were being handled with her new contacts through David C. Cook. You know, people weren't calling her back, and they weren't backing her ideas for promotion. And I said, 'I think if you went to them and just said, "Could you release me from my contract?" they might go along with it.' Because David C. Cook handled mostly children's books. That was their forte. And they did. They released her from our three-book contract."

"After the first two, that was."

"Yeah. And so on she went to Viking/Penguin. Unfortunately, we had our horse shot out from under us. It was kind of a tragic story."

From the original *Blowing Rocket* drawings to those in the Lion editions, Father Tim's severe looks soften, his hair making a miraculous comeback and his glasses growing less prominent on his face.

But it is in the Viking/Penguin versions of the early books that Mitford and Father Tim are fully realized. The drawings show Father Tim about to get knocked ass-over-teakettle, fending off a joyful attack by Barnabas the dog; Father Tim astride his new motor scooter, the townsfolk gathered around to cheer his bravery; Father Tim and Emma, the church secretary, frowning over one of the boxes containing the office computer; Father Tim in the barber chair, about to be shorn by the slightly slutty Fancy Skinner. To observe the progression from weekly paper to small publisher to major house is to witness a franchise being born.

Jan Karon has taken her lumps along the way. She's seen as a saleswoman first and a writer second. She's "a marketing wizard" who's "every bit as sincere as she is slick," according to *Newsweek*. Her books aren't generally reviewed by the big newspapers. And when she does receive attention from a major source, she probably wishes she hadn't. "The promise of [an] easy union with the divine is a large part of what has made Karon successful," opined *The Atlantic*. "But authentic or not, it strikes this [reviewer] as Sunday-school religion: memorize a Bible verse and get a Jesus sticker. . . . The Mitford books are short on wit, poetry, and insight. . . . They seem . . . like children's books for adults."

True, the books touch on unpleasantries like child abuse, illness, and alcoholism, but there's never a doubt everything will be rosily resolved by the last page. *Kirkus* has called them the "literary equivalent of comfort food." Take up a Mitford book after an overnight rest and it's confounding to try to remember the last thing that happened in yesterday's reading.

Then again, there aren't many critics who've invigorated an entire category of literature—Christian fiction. Karon identified a void in the marketplace, and a public hungry for clean, gentle novels marched forth to buy them by the armload.

In many cases, they marched all the way to Blowing Rock, where they roamed the village vainly trying to tie local people and places to their Mitford equivalents. Initially, the Main Street merchants—the same sort of people trusting enough to leave a stranger locked alone in the newspaper office—obliged when asked for directions to the author's cottage, easily identified by the "Peter Rabbit Slept Here" sign outside. Karon suffered so many fans camping on her lawn and otherwise straying beyond the bounds of propriety that she had to establish a primary residence elsewhere.

The merchants have since learned their lesson, though. And the author is forgiving. She returns often.

I'm half-dozing one Saturday morning after the long

drive to my writers' group meeting. It is the portion of the program when the guests in attendance briefly introduce themselves. It usually holds little interest for me. They've written some stories and are trying to find an agent, or they've entered the first two chapters of their novel in a contest, or they're working on some poems and need direction and support.

The woman sitting next to me is new. She's in her sixties and plainly dressed in an old windbreaker. I don't notice much about her beyond her hands, which have the kind of toughened fingertips and well-worn nails that don't clean up even when they're carefully washed. She works in the dirt. She's a farm woman or a serious gardener.

When it's her turn to speak, I sit up straight. Her name is Joan Medlicott, and she's the coauthor of a book called *Celibate Wives: Breaking the Silence.*

I've never spoken to the woman, yet I already know more about her than I should.

The publisher generated little publicity for the book, she says, yet she knocked on doors herself until she was invited to be a guest on *Good Morning America* and other such shows. She's also written a couple of self-published collections of Virgin Islands tales.

I'm not sure I've heard this last part right. I have no idea how to reconcile folklore and sexless marriages.

Joan pays the fee to join the writers' group but to my knowledge doesn't attend any further meetings. Still, she must keep in contact in some fashion, because the news circulates six months or so later that Joan has scored a contract with St. Martin's for a series of woman senior-citizen buddy novels set in the Asheville area. Again, this choice of subject matter is hard to square with her previous work.

I've ordered many books from out-of-print dealers and never felt compelled to explain my purpose until now. "I need a book you have called *Celibate Wives*," I tell the lady over the phone, then quickly add, "I'm doing some background research on one of the coauthors, Joan Medlicott, who now writes novels for St. Martin's."

I don't read much popular psychology, but I'm impressed with the book's even-handed treatment of its subject, and especially with Joan's willingness to open the text with her own case history, in which she frankly discusses her failed sexual expectations following her marriage at age eighteen, the frustration that drove her into an extramarital affair, and finally her divorce after three children and more than fifteen years. She does all this without laying blame on the man she still acknowledges as a good husband generally and a fine father and provider. Clearly, this is a woman with some starch to her.

Joan was born in St. Thomas in the Virgin Islands. Her early marriage interrupted her education. She went back to college at twenty-nine, but because she moved frequently for her husband's job—to Chicago, New York, Florida, Switzerland, Germany—she didn't complete her bachelor's in history for ten years. A self-starter, she also took correspondence courses in horticulture. By the time she returned to St. Thomas in 1964, she knew enough about tropical plants to be hired as director of the Division of Beautification for the Virgin Islands. She remarried in 1967 and earned a master's in counseling while living in Florida in 1973.

After Joan had worked as a therapist for a dozen years, she and a colleague discussed celibacy in their marriages over dinner one night. Knowing the lack of literature on a tender subject that affected some of their clients, they placed ads in local and national publications seeking the stories of women living in sexless marriages. They also raised the subject discretely with the hygienists at the dentist's office, fellow diners at restaurants, and other unsuspecting folk. And so Joan's writing career was born, though it was soon to assume a different shape.

She and her husband moved to Barnardsville, a half-hour north of Asheville. Joan was soaking in the bathtub one day when an idea for a novel struck her.

"Well, I don't know what happened," she tells me during a phone conversation. "These pictures kept coming. They just kept coming and coming. And I was working on something else. I had determined to write a novel about the celibate issue. But these ideas just started to come—a conversation, a visualization of the people—and finally I just set everything else aside and started working. And the minute I did, it was channeled. I don't know how else to tell you. And that may sound really odd to people, but I would open up the computer and start to write. I had no plan, I had no plot, I had no idea what was happening, and it just unfolded."

What came to her was the notion of three senior women—cautious, self-doubting Grace Singleton; outspoken Hannah Parrish, a former professional gardener now plagued by physical problems; and fragile, grief-stricken, French-accented Amelia Declose—living in a dreary Pennsylvania boardinghouse. Emotionally scarred, beginning to break down physically, on uncertain terms with what remains of their families, they've lost all sense of usefulness and are becoming wards of the system.

That is, until Amelia responds kindly to a letter from an unknown relative in the North Carolina mountains. They strike up a correspondence; the elderly gentleman grows ill; Amelia receives notification that he has died and left his farmstead to her.

Grace is the only one of the three friends who can drive. They resolve to pack her old station wagon, leave the lives they hate, and remove themselves to the pin-point village of Covington four states away. There, they set about renovating the farmhouse, pursuing new avocations, finding love, working out their relationships with each other, overcoming their children's protests at their new lifestyle, and generally reviving their spirits in the mountain air.

It's a great concept for a series of popular books designed to appeal to mature women. The first installment, *The Ladies of Covington Send Their Love*, comes out in 2000. *The Gardens of Covington, From the Heart of Covington*, and *The Spirit of Covington* follow within two years. Joan's deal is for hardcovers and paperbacks both.

I ask her what it was like to begin writing fiction at age sixty-six. "That must take a certain self-confidence, to believe you could find success after starting so late," I say.

"And a certain lack of attaching age to what you can do," she says. "I don't attach age to it. I may walk slower, I've had trouble with a knee, and I'm careful where I place my feet. And that's okay. But as long as I'm well, and as long as I've got my mind and my fingers, I have to write.

"I think people have different kinds of minds and different belief systems. I'm a person who always began new careers knowing nothing about them but certain that they would unfold, as these stories unfold. I've always been a storyteller. My grandchildren would come to me and say, 'Grandma, tell me a story,' and I would say, 'Give me the name of a character or an animal or something you want to hear about,' and they would say a stone, a troll, a monster, or whatever, and then I would make up a story.'"

"How long did it take you to place the first book?"

"It took about two and a half years to get it in shape. It didn't take long to get an agent. I sent out query letters to twenty-five agents and received twenty-four no's and one yes. So, naturally, you're so grateful to get an agent, you take the agent gladly. And she was an old-timer in the business and placed the first book very quickly with St. Martin's Press. It was a two-book contract to start with. And then they wanted two more books. But I'm not with them anymore. I'm now with Pocket Books."

"And what are your plans from here?"

"There are to be six books," she says. "And now they're talking about a Christmas book, and they're talking about a cookbook, and they're talking about a gardening book. And I don't want to write fluff, do you know what I mean? So if I write a gardening book, it will be where I take individual kinds of gardens that Hannah would make, and then I do everything—I discuss how to do the soil, I discuss the entire thing from the bottom up—because, you know, part of my background is horticulture. So there would have to be some meat to it."

"That's an opportunity not many people come across," I say.

"You're right. So I'm going to leave that to those people up there to make those kinds of decisions. And I'm flexible at this point because I have three other novels finished that are not Covington novels. And Pocket Books bought one of those novels."

"Is it a stand-alone?"

"Yes, and then I have two others finished. I cannot believe my own productivity, okay? And I'm almost a hundred pages into another novel.

"You know what I would say to writers? 'Persist. Keep on doing it. If you're using a computer, what difference does it make if the first sentence you write ends up on page 92 or 150 at some later date? Just begin, and keep writing, and keep improving.' "

I remark on the thematic similarity between her Covington books and Ann B. Ross's Miss Julia novels. Though they're far apart in tone, both series revolve around women who are empowered late in life. They're about mature women having to learn new skills.

"And Ann Ross is very much a Southern woman herself," Joan says. "She has taught for years at the university, she's married to a doctor, she's lived in the Hendersonville area, and I think that she can speak intimately of the Southern experience. I'm an outsider. I can put outsiders into a Southern environment, and I can draw Southern characters, but I cannot be in the head of a Southern woman."

Ann B. Ross is so much in the head of her Southern woman, Julia Springer of the fictional mountain town of Abbotsville, North Carolina, that people confuse the creator and her creation.

"I'm forever getting that question, 'Aren't you Miss Julia?' " Ross tells me. "But no, I really am not. Maybe I would like to be. And I'm amazed at how many people say they know a Miss Julia—their mother, their aunt, their next-door neighbor. She's a composite, I think, of qualities that a lot of us recognize."

"Do you feel an obligation to play the part?" I ask. "Miss Julia is a pistol. It seems to me it would be difficult to give a reading."

"Oh, bless your heart. No, I tell you, I enjoy it. It really takes it out of me because I get full of adrenaline when I have to speak. But a little bit of classroom experience I suppose helps. But no, I don't play the part. In fact, I make a very strong point that I am not Miss Julia. She says things that I can hardly dare think, so I guess she's my alter-ego, if anything. But when I go out and fifty, seventy, ninety people show up at seven o'clock at night, and I realize what efforts they've made to come out, I just feel I need to entertain them. And I talk about how the ideas came to me, and just try to have a good time, but I don't pretend to be Miss Julia by any means."

At the opening of the first novel, *Miss Julia Speaks Her Mind*, Miss Julia is flipping through a Christmas catalog one August morning when she receives a knock on the door of her home in Abbotsville. It is a young woman with too-yellow hair who's wearing too-high heels and a too-short dress. With her is a nine-year-old boy with a runny nose and a clip-on bow tie. The woman, Hazel Marie, says he is the illegitimate son of Miss Julia's late husband, produces a birth certificate that confirms the fact, instructs Miss Julia to look after the boy while she is away attending beauty school, and speeds off.

Miss Julia has only recently found her husband dead in the driveway, slumped over the wheel of his Buick. During their marriage, he had encouraged her dependency, so she was completely ignorant of the family finances. Now, when she should be settling peacefully into her later years, she unexpectedly finds herself the steward of a small fortune and a bastard boy, the latter a great embarrassment in her church-centered existence.

The series is played for laughs, Miss Julia's sharp-tongued grit-lit narration overlaying incidents that veer into slapstick. In one novel, the boy, Little Lloyd, is kidnapped, and Miss Julia, her black housemaid, and Lloyd's bruised and battered mother, Hazel Marie, have to rescue him from a greedy televangelist during a broadcast. In another, Hazel Marie is kidnapped, and Miss Julia finds herself in a chase on a NASCAR speedway.

There's considerable overlap between Jan Karon's readership and Ann B. Ross's, despite the divergent attitudes toward organized religion in their books.

"Ever since Elmer Gantry polluted the waters . . . [ministers in novels are] all running off with the choir director or doing something worse," Karon remarked to the *Orlando Sentinel*. "Father Tim is an ordinary human being, a decent human being."

If it were possible to find them on a map of the North Carolina mountains, Mitford and Abbotsville would be neighbors, yet Father Tim's species is unknown in Ann B. Ross's town. Miss Julia's spiritual leader, Pastor Ledbetter of First Presbyterian Church, plots ways to gain control of her money. Meanwhile, Brother Vern Puckett, the televangelist, pursues the same money through his blood relationship with Hazel Marie and Little Lloyd, who he feels is due an inheritance from Miss Julia's late husband.

"Your ministers and church people tend to be bad guys," I say to Ross. "How much of that is tongue-in-cheek and how much is real feeling on your part?"

"I've noticed that myself and done it, I suppose, sort of unconsciously," she says. "It's sort of a theme running through it. I am a Christian, and I've been associated with a church all my life, but I've seen a lot of different preachers, some of them very rigid, very dogmatic. 'I've got all the answers.' And they don't. I've been with a church that has split twice. So I'm sure a lot of things that I maybe would have liked to say are coming out in the books."

"Are you active currently? If so, I'm wondering how your fellow church members react to the books."

"Most of my life, I was a Presbyterian. And a few years back, I changed. I'm now an Episcopalian. You know, I live in a small town, so word always gets back to me if anybody says anything. After the first book was published, I heard that everybody in the Presbyterian church was mad at me. And that really kind of made me feel bad, because it was not aimed that way. I used Presbyterianism because it was the one I knew the best, so I didn't have to do any research. But then I felt a whole lot better when somebody told me that another woman in town said, 'Ann says it's the Presbyterians she's writing about, but I know it's the Methodists.' And so that's exactly what I wanted people to see, that there are greedy preachers and gossiping parishioners in any place you've got human beings."

Ann's first books were a pair of what she calls "little murder mysteries set in Charleston."

"I was very, very fortunate to have the very first thing I wrote published, and then to have the second one immediately published," she tells me. "But I still didn't think I knew what I was doing. My children were then well into school, and so I went back to graduate school and got a master's and a Ph.D."

Then came a mainstream novel, *The Pilgrimage.* "I wrote it in one summer, between semesters, but then I got busy researching a dissertation and didn't do anything until I started on Miss Julia."

Like Joan Medlicott, Ann is a writers' group graduate.

When Joan resolved to take up novel writing, she approached it with the same clear purpose she did her other careers, taking classes, hiring an editor, reading copiously, and disregarding the professionals who told her she shouldn't switch from nonfiction to fiction. "When I meet any of those writers' group people somewhere, they have their mouths open, because they cannot believe that somebody who was the worst in the group could get published," Joan tells me.

Ann started with her group, the Wordwrights, after her dissertation interrupted her published writing.

"The reason that the Wordwrights were of such help to me on that first Miss Julia book was that I had lost all contact with any editors or agents or anything, and I did not know where the story was going, and so I was writing sort of when the mood struck me, or when I was supposed to have a chapter to turn in to the group. So I was going very slowly, because I just did not know what it was going to do. And so they gave me a great deal of help on that."

"Was it strictly a ladies' group?" I ask.

"Well, it started out with some men, but it kind of gradually got down to about six or eight of us when we were really getting serious about it."

"People dropped by the wayside?"

"Yes. When it first started, there must have been close to fifteen. And then, very quickly, they realized that the core of us were not there to make people feel good about themselves."

Ann left the group following her first Miss Julia.

"After that was accepted and published, and I was working under a contract and had to have a book a year, I was going too fast to really get a lot of help from them."

Writing three or four hours per morning seven days a week, she now turns out a four-hundred-page manuscript in a little over half a year.

Initially, Joan Medlicott's Covington ladies plan to spend most of the year at their boardinghouse in Pennsylvania and travel to the North Carolina mountains for the summer. But renovations on the Covington farmhouse go so well that they see new possibilities. They realize that, for senior women, the company of peers is more important than the approval of their children. There's nothing that their caretaker in Pennsylvania provides that they can't do for each other. They resolve to pool their resources and move to the mountains year-round. Amelia will supply the residence, thanks to the elderly gentleman's bequest. Hannah's monthly income is fifteen hundred. Grace has twenty-one hundred per month. Hannah will plant a vegetable garden, an herb garden, and a flower garden. Amelia will take up photography, a lifelong interest never pursued. Grace, the nurturer, will repair to the kitchen to fix her special dish, Meatballs and Prunes.

Meatballs and what?

The dish comes up again a hundred pages later. Grace is on poor terms with her gay son, Roger, who wants her to sell her rental property and split the money with him. He entices her back to Pennsylvania by saying how much he'd enjoy a taste of his favorite dish. Though she's fearful of flying and suspicious of his motives, she can't resist the call to Meatballs and Prunes. Soon after arriving, she learns that the real reason Roger summoned her is to break the news that his lover, Charles, has HIV. The health-conscious couple has gone vegetarian, thereby defeating Grace's ball-rolling plans.

But only briefly. Back in Covington, she prepares the dish monthly for Hannah and Amelia, as well as on special occasions.

To make Meatballs and Prunes, you push a prune into the center of each meatball and make sure it's covered on all sides. In principle—and in the wallop delivered—it's like packing snowballs with big chunks of gravel. You roll the meatballs in breadcrumbs, brown them, and then simmer them in a pot with water, tomato paste, onions, and, yes, more prunes.

I learn these details from Joan's website. I also learn from the website that Grace likes the meatballs with rice. Hannah prefers them with potatoes and Amelia with noodles.

Popular mainstream women's writers like Joan Medlicott know how to take care of their readers. Besides Meatballs and Prunes, the website offers recipes for Grace's Multicolored Vienna Cake, Cold Zucchini Soup, Cheesy Cauliflower Bake, Apple Oat Bran Muffins, and Avocado and Pineapple Dip. It also includes biographical material on Joan; a schedule of her appearances; information on large-print editions; synopses of the novels; reader's guides; a map of Covington; photos of Joan with some of her fan clubs; review excerpts; readers' testimonials; personal statements from Grace, Hannah, and Amelia, Amelia's addressed to "*Mes amis*"; and contact information for Joan.

"Let me put it this way: I am accessible," Joan tells me. "On the back of my books is my address and e-mail. People can contact me. There's no mystery. The minute I get a letter from somebody, I answer it immediately. I just sent out a mass mailing to people in my address book, letting them know that the third book is coming out in paperback this month, and the fourth book is coming out in hardback. I have been deluged with mail. People say, 'How kind of you to think of me' and 'Thank you for not forgetting me.' People write me for recipes. Even though they're in the books, they still write, and I will immediately send them a copy, gladly."

Ann B. Ross's website has tips for writers and outlines of future Miss Julia books.

But Jan Karon puts out the best supplementary material for readers.

In her newsletter, *More from Mitford*, you can learn what Jan is reading.

You can also find out what movies she and her daughter are watching.

You can read about the real-life village of Mitford, England, a third the size of the fictional town but just as quirky and quaint.

You can meet the good folks who make Mitford quilts; who write poems about Mitford; who bake Esther Bolick's Orange Marmalade Cake, the series' signature dish; who read their children the Mitford books as part of their home-school curriculum; and who dress up like characters Miss Sadie, Winnie Ivey, Cynthia, Father Tim, Olivia Davenport, and Esther Cunningham to hold a Primrose Tea.

Like the books themselves, the supplementary material is mostly fun but occasionally poignant. You'll meet a woman in the final stages of cancer, a wife with multiple myeloma, and a lady recovering from hip replacement, all of whom take solace in Mitford. Indeed, by means of electronic bulletin boards, the series' fans have fashioned a long-distance support group in the very image of Mitford, a town that doesn't exist.

Of course, there are sales opportunities to be had, too. Readers of the Mitford newsletter are encouraged to purchase not only the principal volumes but also holiday boxed sets; children's books by Jan; *Patches of Godlight: Father Tim's*

Favorite Quotes, supposedly recorded in Father Tim's own handwriting; and Mitford-themed Hallmark merchandise.

Publishers like popular mainstream women's writers for the same reason seniors like Meatballs and Prunes: they move product. But that's not to say profit is what mainly drives the authors.

"It is my intention to give my readers a sense of hope," Jan Karon once told a public-radio interviewer. "I want my readers to love this town and love these people. To go away from their heartache and go into this town and find it real. People ask me, 'Is Mitford real?' My answer is, 'Yes, Mitford is real.' And you know why? It is simply a town where people still care about each other and where old values still work. I live in a town like that, so I know it is real."

CHAPTER 11

The Worthies' Parade

Over time, I quit traveling to my writers' group meetings. There comes a point when I need to do more writing and less hobnobbing. Once I have a firm deadline, I can't afford to give up any more Saturdays. Moreover, since beginning my book, I'm on my third decrepit, high-mileage car, this one farther down the path to the boneyard than the others ever got. On my last trip to the mountains—to Blowing Rock to look at old issues of the *Rocket*, then south on the Blue Ridge Parkway for a publication party and autographing in Asheville—my would-be chariot overheated so badly that I had to shut it down three or four times and wait for it to cool. It has a leaking head gasket, I'm told. It can limp around town, but I'm afraid to run it hard.

Even though I'm absent in body, I pay the dues to maintain my membership, which enables me to keep in touch with my friends' doings via the minutes of the meetings.

For nearly a year and a half, the members comprise a nomadic tribe. One month, I read in the minutes that the group must find a new space, since the branch library that hosts the meetings will be undergoing renovations. The first temporary quarters is a place I've never heard of called the Unity Center, near the airport. Following that, the group meets for several months in the downstairs community room at the library in Weaverville, north of Asheville. Then comes a full year at the fire station in Skyland, a stone's throw from the branch library being upgraded. You park in the lot with the flagpole, I read, and then ring the buzzer at the door on the right and take the elevator located to the right through the second set of doors.

The group holds together just fine through the moves. In fact, attendance is higher than when I used to go. There's talk of putting out a newsletter in addition to the minutes, of starting a group website, and of sponsoring a group table at events at the Asheville Mall and the Grove Arcade. Eileen Johnson reveals at one meeting that the group's origins can be traced to the Blue Ridge Romance Writers back in 1981 or 1982. The next month brings word that one of the founding members is writing a history of the group. Though this doesn't promise scintillating reading, it does speak to the group's spirit, longevity, and closeness.

The members submit their poems, stories, articles, memoirs, and novels to contests, magazines, agents, major houses, regional companies, and self-publishing printers. They report back on book fairs, conferences, and seminars they've attended in Virginia, Tennessee, Kentucky, Georgia, St. Petersburg, Key West, Chicago, Iowa, Maui, and elsewhere. They sign their books whenever the opportunity presents itself and drum up what publicity they can.

The new blood includes a community-college instructor working on a children's book series, a budding suspense novelist who used to write scripts for Hollywood, and a partner in the eatery located next to the Weaverville library. What the restaurateur writes isn't quite clear to me, but I do know from the minutes that at least one longtime member can vouch for her lasagna. Later, I read that, as part of National Novel Month, she's completed a fifty-thousand-word manuscript in thirty days. There's also a Thomas Wolfe scholar who's written a book identifying the real people and places in *Look Homeward, Angel* and is trying to find a publisher for her manuscript about Wolfe's Asheville homecoming in 1937. And there's a local native now living in Australia who returns to the North Carolina mountains for part of the year and wants to publish in the United States.

The most interesting newcomer is a man who's written a novel inspired by *Paradise Lost*. He's read three hundred volumes in preparation for the task, having gone so far as to retrace Milton's research on angels.

I read passing mentions of this man over the course of several months. When he finally accepts a turn as taker of the minutes and later becomes part of the rotation, he elevates what for others is mundane reportage into a kind of art. He warms up by lambasting the shortsightedness of editors, quoting from rejection letters received by Kipling, Faulkner, Emily Dickinson, and William Golding. He muses over the definition of an essay. He includes in the minutes an article from a major paper on primary and secondary imagination and the craft of the novelist. He laments the narrowness of the Western canon. He reprints blurbs for a novel by Andrei Codrescu, who will be coming to North Carolina for a conference. He defines the differences among gothic, neo-gothic, and horror fiction. He bemoans the way bookstores divide fiction among genres, since his own novel, despite its classic roots, would likely be banished to the horror section, to be thumbed by raincoat-wearing perverts. When it appears that the money for the branch library's renovation is in danger of being reallocated elsewhere, he lists the county commissioners' addresses and phone numbers and encourages protest.

As does anyone who bares his heart so freely, he occasionally oversteps his bounds. During one meeting, as I understand it, my friend Bryan Aleksich offers advice on avoiding a common computer problem. The newcomer subsequently writes five paragraphs in the minutes explaining how utterly wrong Bryan was, citing his own extensive computer training and ten years' experience in the field. If I've read Bryan's personality correctly, he's more likely to appreciate the knowledge than to take offense at the correction. But all the same, the matter could have been handled better. And though I've never met the man, he gets my blood pumping with this quote from John Gardner he includes in the minutes: "One should fight like the devil the temptation to think well of editors. They are without exception . . . either incompetent or crazy."

Month by month, I follow his quest for publication as it assumes a familiar arc: he's looking for an agent for his novel; he's discouraged by the cost of hiring an editor to get his manuscript into shape; he finds an editor and is invigorated not only by her work but also by her offer to submit the novel to a friend of hers at St. Martin's; he eagerly awaits word from the publisher and begins a sequel in the meantime; his optimism wanes as a month passes, then another; he receives a rejection notice; he sends a batch of queries to other publishers, apparently without much luck; he seems to reconcile himself to print-on-demand or self-publishing.

Print-on-demand technology, a frequent topic of discussion at the writers' group meetings, shows promise of being a great equalizer for the members. My friends envision the day when bookstores will be places where people go to have the books of their choice printed fresh on the spot. When there is no longer a need for standing inventory, the interests that control printing and distribution will no longer hold sway, since it will be as economical to print single copies of books by unknown authors as by John Grisham. Likewise, traditional rejecters like agents and editors will no longer stand between the members and the reading public. A new dawn is at hand.

An exchange of e-mails after one of the meetings shows how swiftly reality hits home. The members have been discussing the costs charged by a couple of print-on-demand publishers. Steve Brown, who apparently did not attend the meeting and is reading the minutes a couple of days later just as I am, knows of a cheaper and better alternative and broadcasts an e-mail to the entire membership.

Jack Pyle sends a reply to Steve, in which he points out the near-impossibility of getting one's print-on-demand titles stocked in chain bookstores and the continuing second-class status of self-published writers.

What follows is a lively debate between the group's two dominant voices—sent to all the members—over the realities of new-technology publishing. Steve says wide distribution of one's print-on-demand books is possible; Jack says it's fantasy. They good-naturedly parse words in each other's e-mails. To Steve, a *buyer* is someone who purchases books for a chain. To Jack, it's someone who buys.

Steve finally clarifies his position by saying it's feasible to get print-on-demand books distributed if you convince the chains you're a serious multibook writer and not a one- or two-book hobbyist. He says one of the main impediments to distribution is the refusal of many self-published authors to seek out editorial help. The result has been a high incidence of poorly written material. He tells of some chain stores where staff members entertain themselves by circulating self-published books in which they're marked all the misspellings and other blunders.

These comments draw fire from a couple of members who are one-book self-published writers but who emphatically *do not* consider themselves hobbyists and who care every bit as much about their craft as any multibook author does.

Steve nimbly pulls his biscuits from the fire while still maintaining his position. He says he certainly wasn't referring to the members in question, but that quality control *is* a serious problem in self-publishing.

Among those who consider the print-on-demand option is Bryan Aleksich, indefatigable as ever.

Bryan and I exchange letters now and then. He sends me tips on material for my new book and magazine clippings related to my old one. He's taken to writing guest editorials, and he occasionally encloses samples of those. When he learns that the Hendersonville paper welcomes only two such editorials a year per writer—a limit he reaches by February—he begins writing for the Asheville paper, too. He submits accompanying illustrations, which are professional enough for the papers to run.

As for his novel, it is named a semifinalist in one national contest and a finalist in another. He pays to have the manuscript scrutinized by three separate editors. He submits a twenty-page sample as part of a writers' conference in Athens, Georgia. It comes to the attention of a senior vice president at Simon & Schuster, who asks to see the entire novel, then passes it to a subordinate. It's returned a month later with a letter telling Bryan how close he came to publication.

In the minutes from one of the writers' group meetings, it's reported that Bryan is hard at work on a dozen novels. This must be mistaken. To my knowledge, his Cold War story is the only one he's ever written. He once told me that, instead of looking in the mirror and seeing someone who's spent thirty-odd years writing a novel, he prefers to view himself as having written a dozen different novels from the same source material. That distinction was apparently lost on the minutes-taker.

Bryan sinks twenty-seven hundred dollars into his print-on-demand venture. But when he receives the proofs, he discovers that his drawing at the front of the book, designed to stretch across the title page and its verso page, has been reduced to fit on the title page only; that the font for his chapter titles has been changed, and is now different from the font for the main text; that the margins are too narrow throughout the book; and that his brief statement at the end of the text describing the type font has been replaced by an author biography, which merely duplicates the author biography on the back flap. He's so upset that he withdraws the entire project.

Not to worry, though. Coming out the other side of triple-bypass surgery, Bryan is ready to begin submitting again. He finds a small publisher in the mountains that is happy to take on his Cold War novel. It's due to be released about the same time as my own book. I hope this will bring a satisfactory end to his decades-long devotion. I have no doubt it's a far better novel now than when he self-published it many years ago and took an electric drill to the unsold copies.

I'm also pleased for Frankie Schelly, who once seemed so frustrated over her efforts at placing her social-issues novels. She finally foots the bill for *At the Crossroads*, which centers around four nuns who teach at a parish school threatened with closing. The writers' group members like the novel but not the page design. Frankie apparently agrees; a couple of months later, I read that she's had it laid out again and reprinted. She then releases another novel, *Chance Place*.

Frankie proves a tireless promoter, as everyone knew she would be once she got started. *At the Crossroads* is favorably reviewed in *Library Journal*, quite a coup for a self-published effort. It wins an honorable mention in a contest sponsored by *Writer's Digest*, while *Chance Place* is a finalist for the International Hemingway First Novel Award—though it's actually her second, by my count. She takes a shot at selling foreign rights at the Frankfurt Book Fair in Germany.

Eileen Johnson continues traveling to Ireland. In fact, her writing inspires a couple of her readers to take trips there, too. After she publishes her regional history tracing Irish roots in Appalachia, and then her Irish cookbook, she undertakes a novel about the potato famine.

Jack Pyle's *The Sound of Distant Thunder*, once submitted to my company in manuscript form, is chosen Novel of the Year by the Appalachian Writers' Association, an award previously won by Robert Morgan, Sharyn McCrumb, and Charles Frazier. Jack is now the author or coauthor of seven books ranging from moon-sign-gardening guides to a mystery novel to a short-story collection to a young-adult novel. He sends me a copy of his latest, largest, and most ambitious novel, *Black Horse, White Rider*, about a New York clergyman's daughter who marries a philandering, slaveholding rice-plantation owner from Georgia.

Steve Brown's energy and creativity in promoting his books are a match for anyone's. He has a series of three James Stuart novels, a pair of World War II novels, and three stand-alone novels. His Susan Chase mysteries now number six. They're sold in stores, of course, but they're also available through his websites, individually or in a complete set, autographed or not. And he's forged a mass-market deal with one of the Simon & Schuster imprints for five of the Susan

Chase books. Moreover, he's savvy enough to have retained rights to the series. He's pleased that he finally has a contract with a major house, but he still takes special pride in hand-selling his original Chick Springs Publishing editions.

I'm browsing a mega-bookstore out of state one day. One of those catch-all tables toward the front is stacked with books organized by no apparent theme—*The Art of War, Candide, Lolita,* Kafka's *Metamorphosis*, David McCullough's biography of John Adams, a Jonathan Franzen, a Barbara Kingsolver, a David Guterson, a Garrison Keillor.

But wait! There's *America Strikes Back*—touted on the cover as "the exciting sequel to *Of Love & War*"—by Steve Brown. Hey, I know that guy!

I think of writing or calling him when I get home, but I let the moment pass. He'd be thrilled to learn his book is keeping such company. Then again, there's a good chance he knows already.

When Charles Price travels on behalf of his novel published by my company, he has middling results.

We finally agree on *Freedom's Altar* as a title. One day, he is to give a reading at a large chain store. The events co-ordinator has set him up a lectern and a small array of chairs for listeners. But an audience is slow to materialize. The chairs have been pilfered from their customary places around the store, and browsers would like to have them back. Someone approaches Charles and asks to take one of the chairs. He's not in a position to say no even if he would. Seeing the first person's success, another customer is emboldened to remove a chair, as is a third. It isn't long before Charles is alone at his lectern with neither listeners nor the means to accommodate them, unless they think to bring floor pillows.

Should he begin reading to the empty space and hope his voice draws someone?

Should he pack his stuff and try to sneak out unnoticed?

The first time he wears his Western getup for a reading is at an independent store of excellent repute. He does have an audience that day, but when he's introduced and stands to begin his presentation, he discovers he's forgotten his glasses and can't read a thing. The lady running the store offers hers, which he gladly accepts, no matter that their predominantly purple color and bright sparkles diminish the effect of his big hat, fancy boots, and shoestring tie.

In Nashville, Tennessee, there's a Confederate cemetery that holds the grave of one of the Curtises, the true-life family on whose lives *Freedom's Altar* is loosely based. Charles's visit to the grave is to be covered by local television. He waits forty minutes at the site, however, and the camera crew never shows.

The shame in all this is that the book is as good as we thought. "Against a fascinatingly detailed backdrop of the decaying and lawless postslavery South," says *Publishers Weekly*, "Price eloquently addresses questions of race and class and morality, poignantly exploring whether hope and loyalty can exist in a world where war has damaged lives irrevocably." *Booklist* finds it "compelling" and "lyrical yet controlled," while *Kirkus* judges it "well-written." It claims the Sir Walter Raleigh Award, the state's highest literary prize, an honor won over its fifty-year history by luminaries from Reynolds Price to John Ehle to Fred Chappell to Lee Smith to Allan Gurganus to Kaye Gibbons to Clyde Edgerton.

Charles sends us a new novel. It's a follow-up to *Freedom's Altar*, and the third of his Price-Curtis novels stretching from the Civil War into Reconstruction.

The manuscript is disappointing. Overly derivative of his previous work, it reexamines scenes from the first two novels and focuses on characters whose wads have been shot. It's heavy on summarizing and explaining at the expense of storytelling, which is Charles's strength. There's none of the delight we got when the manuscript that became *Freedom's Altar* showed up at our door.

Except for one chapter, that is. It tells of the short-lived moonshining career of young Ves Price, the son of one of the principals in *Freedom's Altar*. Ves is the kind of stupid person who's dangerous because of his conviction that he's clever. In the span of about twenty pages, he overcooks the mash, dumps barrels of moonshining by-products into a stream where they can easily be traced to the dangerous men for whom he's working, samples the new batch too liberally, alienates an old girlfriend, and soils himself and exposes his privates in front of his true love. Since we met him as a boy in *Freedom's Altar*, Ves has matured into a worthless, effortless fuckup, and we want to know what further damage he can do.

We reject the manuscript. Using the moonshining chapter as our example, we tell Charles how he should have moved the saga into the next generation of characters and given them their own, new story lines. Should he ever consider doing so, we tell him, he's welcome to send the manuscript back for another look.

We don't hold out much hope. We're really asking for an entirely different novel. We're suggesting he keep twenty pages and throw out four hundred.

What comes back some months later reminds me why I go to work in the morning. Ves Price is still there, but his is only the second- or third-best story line now. The novel really belongs to a minor character from *Freedom's Altar*, Hamby McFee, a headstrong mulatto who doesn't fit among either blacks or whites but who remains bound to the land by a bitter, confused loyalty he wishes he didn't feel. Hamby raises fighting chickens. His dream is to accumulate enough winnings to leave the mountains, while his reality is a life of labor that keeps afloat what remains of the Curtises, the local aristocracy gone to seed. The main thrust of the story is how he comes to accept his feelings for the Curtis clan, the only family he has, even to the extent of putting his life at stake for family friend Ves Price, whose greed has led him to inform on moonshiners for the Revenue, and whose incompetence has gotten him caught doing it.

I've never known an author to take a suggestion and run with it so well, or to turn a book around so completely. It's the best manuscript I've read in my time in the business.

Informally, Charles refers to it as "the chicken book." We publish it as *The Cock's Spur*.

"Lyrically written, character-rich and authentically atmospheric, the novel affords a deeply affecting insight into the aftermath of war," says *Publishers Weekly*. Charles is named Storyteller of the Year at the Independent Publisher Book Awards.

Still, returns of the book are heavy. Reviews are fewer than for *Freedom's Altar*, and save for *Publishers Weekly*, they're in minor magazines and newspapers. Charles now has three novels, each superior to the last, yet his sales are stagnant.

On both sides, there's disappointment. We all feel—*know*—they're good novels that should be finding an audience by now. Charles wishes we had a more sensible plan for promoting his books. Some on our staff wish he were a more enthusiastic salesman. There are no hard feelings, but when Charles writes a fourth and final manuscript in his saga, it's mutually agreed that it's time to part company.

This one is called "Where the Water-Dogs Laughed." *The Cock's Spur* remains my favorite, but there's no doubt the new novel is the most daring thing Charles has written, particularly in the way it pays homage to the Cherokee culture and world view. At its center is Northern exploitation of the Southern mountains, in the person of timber baron George Gordon Meade Weatherby. A full-time clear-cutter of forests and part-time hunter of big game, Weatherby grows obsessed in his quest to kill the preeminent bear in the high country. Wounded in the head and driven to rage by pain, infection, and hunger, the animal turns the attack on his tormentors. It is left to Hamby McFee, now aged, to track and kill the bear in the merciful, grateful tradition of the Cherokees and so begin to restore balance to the natural world. It is Hamby's death scene, too.

As should a man with three well-received novels and a

pair of midlevel awards to his credit, Charles begins by contacting agents in the hope of making a sale to a national publisher. But like me, he's not as persistent as he ought to be. One agent tells him he's "clearly a wonderful writer" who is "fully deserving of representation and a larger potential readership," then declines to take him on as a client because of the difficulty in getting publishers to accept "a writer such as yourself."

What kind of writer would that be, exactly? He's understandably discouraged by such mixed messages.

Charles submits the manuscript directly to an editor at one noted house, only to receive a faux-personal reply saying it has been read "with care and interest"—though his package appears not to have been opened at all—and that it is being rejected because "we are a small publishing company and we have to limit our list to only a few new titles each year." Charles fires off a reply mimicking the letter line by line, describing himself as "a small author" who must limit himself to a few rejections per annum. It's funny and probably justified. It's his way of saying good-bye to commercial concerns, to the whole set of conditions that combine to turn aside good work.

The novel finally finds a home with a new, small publisher in the mountains. The staff there is thrilled to have Charles and promises to involve him in every phase of the process. As a gesture of their developing relationship, the publisher even presents him a three-foot chainsaw-carved figure of a bear.

A couple of times, I try to draw him out on the subject of Charles Frazier.

Feelings in the mountains toward Frazier are complex. When someone like Robert Morgan scores an Oprah-sized coup, it's acknowledged that he's gotten lucky, of course, but the consensus is that he's fought the noble fight over a long career and that his good fortune is to be celebrated. But Frazier's success has so far exceeded everyone else's, and it's come by such a different path, that there's no agreement on what to make of him. He's a man whose manuscript likely would have mildewed in a basement if his wife hadn't taken part of it without his knowledge and shown it to her friend Kaye Gibbons, who in turn recommended it to her agent. He's also a man whose one-page outline for a second novel, based on the life of white Indian Will Thomas—a well-known figure in the mountains whose story anyone might have fictionalized—brought him an eight-million-dollar book deal and another three million for movie rights.

Those who've met Frazier or heard him speak seem to like him. But there's also a great deal of jealousy. I know one author who disparages him rather bitterly as "Dr. Frazier" and feels his fame is wholly due to advantages not enjoyed by working writers. I know another who swears irrationally that Frazier stole his stuff in writing *Cold Mountain*, even though Frazier was solidly within his rights in his use of historical material.

Charles Price would figure to have as much cause as anyone to resent Frazier. They write of the same people in the same locales during the same time frame. They write the same long paragraphs in the same carefully crafted period language.

But Charles Price won't take the bait when I offer it to

him. In fact, when he learns I'm interested in Frazier, he tries to put me in touch via a friend who supposedly knows Frazier's address. Though it comes to nothing, I appreciate the effort. And *Cold Mountain* appears prominently on the reading list Charles Price gives to the people who come to his seminars.

Coincidentally, the release of the *Cold Mountain* movie is only a month or two away when I enter the bookstore that's hosting the publication party for Charles Price's fourth novel. *Cold Mountain* won the Sir Walter Raleigh Award two years before *Freedom's Altar* did.

Coming to the big screen simultaneously with *Cold Mountain* is the Tim Burton movie *Big Fish*, adapted from the novel of the same name by North Carolinian Daniel Wallace. That novel was a nominee for the Sir Walter the year *Freedom's Altar* won.

In a way, I regret that the movies are raining gold all around Charles Price while he collects pennies. But that denies that good writing is a sufficient end unto itself, the very point I've argued to him on several occasions.

I intend to talk with Charles after his presentation and maybe even join him for a bite to eat, but I understand that won't be possible when I see the crush of people. Forty or more of them have come out tonight to pack the small store, and they seem to be familiar with Charles's whole body of writing. Everyone bypasses the free food and drink to get a good seat for the reading.

Since I spoke with her, Sharyn McCrumb has written a couple more of her Ballad novels.

In *The Songcatcher*, she uses her own family history to further some of her favorite themes. It centers around a country singer trying to recollect a song she heard years ago. While traveling home to the Appalachians to be with her dying father, she's trapped inside her small plane when it crashes. Those chapters are alternated with the story of her—and Sharyn's—eighteenth-century ancestor as he makes his way from a Scottish isle to the mountains of western North Carolina. Having learned the song aboard ship, he passes it to his descendants, who in turn teach it to succeeding generations.

But just when you think you know Sharyn well enough to map out the rest of her career, she comes up with the concept for her new novel, to be called *St. Dale*, which will give a nod to *The Canterbury Tales* in following a group of bus-touring NASCAR fans on their pilgrimage to Dale Earnhardt sites.

Fred Chappell has written a couple of new poetry volumes and retired from his teaching job.

Robert Morgan is still quietly adding quality work to the literature, having published a volume of poetry and a pair of novels, the latter of which, *Brave Enemies*, tells of the circumstances that lead a young couple to end up on opposite sides at the Revolutionary War battle at Cowpens, the woman disguised as a boy.

Gail Godwin continues to stretch herself, writing her first nonfiction work, *Heart: A Personal Journey Through Its Myths and Meanings*, and the elegant autobiographical novella *Evenings at Five*, inspired by the passing of her longtime companion, composer Robert Starer.

I still receive automated e-mail updates from Ann B. Ross

and Joan Medlicott, whose Miss Julia and Covington series, respectively, proceed apace. At last word, Miss Julia was trying to decide whether to accept her suitor's marriage proposal, while the Covington ladies were departing the mountains to take a cruise in the Caribbean, their creator's native territory.

And though he's not the biggest name among Asheville-area authors, I'm impressed with the progress of Bill Brooks's career. Bill took on a staggering workload, beginning a new series of genre Westerns and a series of bad-guy literary novels simultaneously, and he's delivered well on both fronts. His latest in the latter series, *Bonnie and Clyde: A Love Story*, is perhaps his best work. For Bill, writing is a learned craft first and a God-given talent second, and his novels are evidence that even a veteran author can make great strides in his skills.

CHAPTER 12

Unfinished Business

I tell my daughters how important it is that they look out for each other, how they'll go much farther as allies than enemies.

I tell them to be sure to take care of their mother.

When it's their time, they should choose boys who care about them and have a future. Character and intelligence are more important than style and looks.

I tell my daughters that, all our petty squabbles not-withstanding, they've never disappointed me.

I tell them they should never doubt their ability, and that all possibilities are open to them depending on their willingness to work.

I've cornered them at bedtime, so they're groggy and a little slow on the uptake. But they're bright kids, and I can see the recognition begin to hit them. If I've got such great advice, they're thinking, then why haven't I followed it to success and happiness myself?

"You're just taking a plane ride, Dad," one of them says.

But the next afternoon at the Asheville airport, it appears my vision of an early death may not be far-fetched.

First, Mike, my pilot, can't get his door open. I see him through the windows from where I'm stooped under the wing on the passenger side. He rattles the handle, then starts pulling on it hard. Mike's a big, strong guy, and the whole plane shakes slightly. It's thirty or forty seconds before the latch finally gives.

And then another light plane—identical to the one we'll be flying—taxis into the spot just beyond us. Mike leaves off his preflight check and looks on quizzically as the other pilot shuts down, gets out, and approaches with his flight student in tow.

"A screw from the engine cowling came flying off on takeoff," he informs Mike. "I had to bring us back in."

And then, when we're at the end of the taxiway ready to be cleared for takeoff, we're told to wait while a maintenance vehicle examines the runway for the lost engine-cowling screw. We look left and, sure enough, a pickup truck speeds down the runway with its lights flashing. It must be doing fifty, way too fast to spot an object as small as a screw—which indeed it doesn't.

"Something like that could pop a tire on landing," Mike says matter-of-factly.

While we're waiting, he mentions that the turbulence can get pretty strong close to the mountains.

"Try to give me a little notice if you feel you're going to be sick," he says.

A friendship between two of the most unlikely writers in the South began in 1948, when Harry Golden was among a small group of reporters who came to Connemara to interview seventy-year-old Carl Sandburg and then escort him to a speech.

When he later returned to Connemara for a private interview, Golden was nervous, not wanting to present himself as the kind of newspaperman who asked mundane questions about how Sandburg enjoyed living in North Carolina and about what he was presently writing. To break the ice, he presented a bottle of whiskey as a gift. Sandburg was so delighted that it thereafter became a tradition for guests to bring him whiskey—and for Sandburg to make a show of having glasses carried in, which he filled not with the whiskey but with goat's milk from his wife's herd. He got a laugh at people's reactions. Most of them bravely drank.

Harry Golden stayed a full eight hours at Connemara that day. Sandburg kissed him on both cheeks when he left.

The Ukrainian-born, New York-raised Golden had moved to North Carolina in 1941 and soon thereafter started a conventional small newspaper in Charlotte. Unhappy with his efforts after a couple of years, he decided to remake that paper, the *Carolina Israelite*, in the form of a personal journal. Save for the section of letters to the editor, he wrote the whole thing himself, fifteen thousand to twenty-five thousand words a month. It contained no news; the only obituary he ran,

Golden liked to tell people, treated the assassination of Julius Caesar in 44 B.C. Rather, each issue was a collection of editorials covering everything from Jewish culture to New York politics to Southern attitudes to ancient civilizations. These drew on Golden's massive reading in history, literature, and philosophy, but all his writing was off the top of his head, as he never left his chair to consult any other person's work or any reference book. He wrote on random subjects as the spirit took him and pitched his finished pages into a barrel, from which he would draw a selection when it came press time.

This may sound like an amateurish way to run a paper, but that underestimates Golden's intelligence, wit, and writing skills. Among his fourteen thousand subscribers nationwide were a good many influential people. Golden once attended a session of the House Un-American Activities Committee and was dismayed—and maybe secretly proud— to note that all eight witnesses called were *Israelite* subscribers. His editorial outlining the "Golden Vertical Negro Plan" is a classic humorous antisegregation piece. Indeed, Martin Luther King identified Golden as one of four white journalists whose work played a significant role in the civil-rights movement.

Golden was rotund and liked fat cigars. The rail-thin Carl Sandburg was so frugal that he cut his thin stogies in half and smoked them so low that it looked like his lips were smoldering. Other than that, the bleeding-heart Jew and the battle-toughened old socialist had a great deal in common.

Mike takes us around Connemara in a low circle— clockwise, so my side is banked low and I have the better view. The place is beautiful in springtime, from the dammed lake at the base of the property to the front porch where Sandburg and Golden met. Beyond the main structure is the steep-roofed "Swedish House," to which Sandburg exiled the books that overflowed his six-thousand-square-foot home. Some distance beyond that is the goat barn. I can't see the mountain trails the two friends walked during Golden's frequent visits, when Sandburg would leave the man twenty-four years his junior puffing in his wake.

In 1958, Golden put together a book of his editorials culled from the *Israelite*. In acknowledgment of the run of success by which a transplanted Jew had become the best-known man in his corner of the South, he called it *Only in America*. Sandburg wrote the foreword. Books of warmed-over newspaper columns almost always sell poorly, but Golden's became a number-one bestseller. Even today, decades after it should be badly outdated, its insightful snippets of culture, history, and local color still make it one of the all-time-great bathroom reads.

And then the roof fell in—or should have. Someone sent an anonymous letter to his New York publisher asking, "Do you know that your author . . . is a swindler, a cheat, and an ex-con and jail bird who has victimized widows and orphans?"

It was true. The man known as Harry Golden was Herschele Lewis Goldhirsch, who had started a New York brokerage in the mid-1920s and declared bankruptcy within a few years, at which time he was unable to return his clients' investments following unsuccessful market speculation. He pled guilty to mail fraud and stock manipulation and spent three years in prison—where he began to develop his journalistic skills editing the jailhouse rag.

It's unclear how far Golden discussed this with Sandburg, who'd done some jail time himself when he was caught hopping a train in his hoboing days. Sandburg most likely would have ascribed Golden's offense to youthful indiscretion.

In any case, Golden again defeated the odds by parlaying the scandal into greater fame.

Though Sandburg is credited with coining the phrase *idiot box*, he and his guitar had been television favorites since the mid-1950s. Many consider Sandburg to have had the largest public persona of any American author save Mark Twain. Harry Golden didn't have a passable singing voice and a repertoire of one-chord songs like his mentor, but he, too, became a TV figure, appearing regularly with Jack Paar on *The Tonight Show*.

In 1961, Golden published a biography of Sandburg. The same editorialist's sensibility that made the *Carolina Israelite* and *Only in America* such successes doomed the biography to mediocrity. Partly a chronological account of Sandburg's life, partly a generous overview of his poetry, the book is mainly a grab bag of disconnected anecdotes. Its usefulness is only as a supplement to serious works on Sandburg. Golden would have been wise to leave his chair long enough to do some hard research with a view toward organizing a continuous work.

Not far east of us is Tryon, where F. Scott Fitzgerald came to dry out at least a couple of times between 1935 and 1937. Local people will tell you he stayed at the Pine Crest Inn, though some written sources say it was the Oak Hall Hotel, no longer in business.

"Shall we head over in that direction?" Mike asks. "It's only a few minutes."

Sensitive to running over my hour's time and incurring costs I can't afford, I decline.

Mike may sense this pressure on me. He points to a large, grand structure on a hill some distance away. "Could that be it?"

Probably not. The Pine Crest is green with a white roof, and the main inn isn't particularly large, most of the guest rooms being in the eight or so cottages scattered around the property. Though there's a Fitzgerald Room in one of the other cottages, Fitzgerald is believed to have stayed in the 1760s-vintage Swayback Cottage. It may have been there that Thomas Wolfe visited him on his return to the Asheville area in 1937. Ernest Hemingway is said to have stayed in the Swayback, too, perhaps having come for the same reason as Fitzgerald. That visit is even harder to pin down.

For such a pretty place, the Tryon area has drawn notable writers for all the wrong reasons. Just a few miles farther east is the home where Georgia poet Sidney Lanier came to die in 1881 at the age of thirty-nine, of the tuberculosis that had dogged him since he contracted it in a prison camp during the Civil War.

Instead of heading east from Connemara, we make the momentary jog west to Hendersonville.

In November 1935, Fitzgerald came to Hendersonville and took a room at the Skyland Hotel. "It was funny," he wrote, "coming into the hotel and the very deferential clerk not knowing that I was not only thousands, nay tens of thousands in debt, but had less than 40 cents cash in the world and probably a $13 deficit at my bank." He washed his own laundry and subsisted on canned food.

It was at the Skyland that winter that he wrote his "Crack-Up" series of articles. The three confessional pieces, published in *Esquire* in early 1936, detailed his emotional emptiness and the downward spiral of his creative powers. Though they were the best writing of his later years, his public admission that he was a broken man only served to further damage his reputation.

The hotel building still stands on Main Street, though it has been converted to other uses.

Mike comes low and circles over Hendersonville's Oakdale Cemetery and the famous Wolfe Angel—a marble angel from the monument shop of Thomas Wolfe's father, said to be the inspiration for the central image in *Look Homeward, Angel*. I knew of its existence but had forgotten all about it until Mike reminded me.

Mike and I seem to be kindred spirits. He's lived in the area for only a few years and seems genuinely interested to hear my stories of famous authors. And for my part, I envy people in his line of work. Years ago, Mike was one of those kids flying banner-dragging planes at the beach. He put himself through aeronautical college and got certified all the way up through good-sized corporate jets, all on his own dime. He now flies a good many business charters.

"I just like flying," he tells me, "whether it's high and fast or low and slow."

I'd hire him and his plane for the entire afternoon if I could. He's flattened out the countryside for me and finally given me some perspective on a place that's proven hard to grasp from ground level. Moreover, it's a pleasure dealing with someone who loves his work and is good at it. He's long since put me at ease. He interrupts our conversation only to talk to the controllers. He guides the plane with his left hand and uses the right to dial in new course headings and punch in radio codes and to point things out to me.

On our way north to Asheville, we pass east of and parallel to the runway from which we departed forty minutes ago. I remark that it looks awfully long for a town Asheville's size. Mike chuckles. He tells me that it measures eight thousand feet and is designated an alternate landing site for the space shuttles, though it has never been put to that use. But a Concorde actually landed here once and was stranded for three days because of the snow, he says.

The Biltmore Estate lies near the south edge of town.

"I can circle here all day if you like," Mike says.

I'm inclined to move onward.

I don't think he minds a bit, as he's no doubt done Biltmore many times.

Mike is unfamiliar with Riverside Cemetery, where Wolfe and O. Henry are buried, but he picks it out quickly when I tell him it lies along the French Broad River north of the center of town. I'm unused to identifying things from this height. I do well enough with major sites like Biltmore and the distant, orange-roofed Grove Park Inn, but in some cases there's a lag of fifteen or twenty seconds from the time Mike spots what I'm looking for until it finally comes clear to me. Though the trees are fully out, the cemetery is much more sparsely vegetated than I thought. It looks as deserted today as every time I've been there by car.

Just five or six blocks farther out Montford Avenue is the former site of Highland Hospital. I don't know the area well enough to pick out much from the air, except for some of the old structures bordering the taller, newer Mountain Area Hospice that were probably part of the hospital. There's really not much to see from the ground either, save for a portion of the stone steps of the building that burned and a small marker by the porte-cochere of Highland Hall on Zillicoa Street.

"I don't need anything except hope, which I can't find by looking backwards or forwards. So I suppose the thing to do is to shut my eyes," the inscription on the marker reads, a quote from Zelda Fitzgerald.

Zelda lived such a complex, eventful, sad life that it's possible to select something from it to buttress just about any point you care to make. She can be interpreted to mean many different things. For me, her time in Asheville says something about the indomitability of the artistic spirit.

Born in July 1900, Zelda was four years younger than her husband and two and a half months older than Thomas Wolfe. As the original flapper and a woman whose mission it was to test cultural boundaries, she lived a life that had the status of public art—or at least spectacle. But she reached a point in her late twenties when, wanting to see whether any substance lay behind her style, she resolved to draw out whatever talent she had. She put so much pressure on herself to make up for her frivolous years, and her efforts were such a bitter issue in her marriage, that her desire to create art was one of the factors that pushed her into mental illness.

By the time Scott checked her into Highland Hospital in April 1936, Zelda was a shell of a human being. She had suffered nervous collapses, made numerous suicide attempts, and been hospitalized in Paris, Switzerland, Baltimore, and New York. Her troubles had been variously diagnosed as nervous exhaustion, religious mania, severe depression, and schizophrenia. She had hallucinations, heard voices, suffered delusions, experienced homosexual yearnings, and believed she communicated with Jesus, Apollo, and William the Conqueror.

In Europe in the early 1930s, she was given ovarian extracts, thyroid-gland powders, and potassium bromide. She was injected with her own blood, with a serum made from the brain of a mentally fit person, with morphine to bring sleep, with belladonna for pain, with luminal for sedation. She submitted to the "Swiss Sleeping Cure," according to which she received morphine and bromides rectally, which immediately brought about narcosis for two weeks. One of the treatment's side effects was eczema on her neck and face and in her eye sockets so severe that she was confined to bed for five weeks on one occasion. A famously vain woman, Zelda had her face swaddled in bandages and her hands bound to stop her compulsive masturbating.

During her institutionalization in the United States in the mid-1930s, she was given stramonium for mania, digitalis as an antidepressant, and chloral hydrate and sodium amytal as tranquilizers. Her Metrazol convulsive treatments induced epileptic-type seizures so severe that she had to be held down so she wouldn't fracture her hips, spine, or jaw.

Scott brought her to Asheville partly because the care at Highland Hospital was cheaper than at her previous institution. It cost twelve hundred dollars a quarter, but Scott claimed hard times and paid only a little over half that. He took her to lunch at the Grove Park Inn on occasion.

Under Dr. Robert Carroll, Highland had a reputation for progressive treatment. Carroll recruited his staff from the ranks of the "cured." He was the author of popular books on the treatment of nervous disease and also of an autobiographical novel about a caring young doctor. He believed that mental illness could be controlled through diet and exercise. Like the other hospital residents, Zelda was forbidden alcohol, tobacco, drugs, and rare meat and was allowed few sweets. She played volleyball and did calisthenics in the mornings and walked up and down a nearby hill a certain number of times a day, as prescribed by Dr. Carroll.

Beneath that veneer, however, the treatment was more horrific than ever. Zelda took injections of honey, hypertonic solutions, placental blood, and horse blood, the latter of which induced aseptic meningitis. She also underwent a therapy that combined insulin shock and electroshock. During insulin-shock therapy, patients were given insulin injections to bring about hypoglycemic shock and coma. The more profound the coma—so the theory went—the greater the number of "sick neurons" in the brain were killed. The goal was to induce fifty to a hundred such comas over a three-month period. Electroshock involved the firing of 180 to 460 volts of electricity through the brain from temple to temple or from front to back on one side, the object being to induce grand-mal convulsions. The typical treatment was twenty consecutive shocks three times a week.

What emerged from all of this was a completely different person. Zelda's attractiveness had always been a product more of flair than beauty, but now she was prematurely aged and homely. More importantly, the woman who was once the foremost socialite of her generation was no longer able to function in society.

It's hard to guess what Zelda might have become under different circumstances. Her greatest love was ballet. Though she didn't take it up until the age of twenty-seven, she still possessed enough ability to have made herself a modest professional career. But that prospect only maddened her.

As for her writing, Scott considered her a third-rate talent—and told her so—yet made use of passages from her letters and diaries in his own work. Her mental illness, thinly disguised, was put forward for public consumption in *Tender Is the Night*, but when she sought to treat their marriage in her own novel, Scott tried to suppress her efforts. By some accounts, that 1932 novel of Zelda's, *Save Me the Waltz*, was also sabotaged by Maxwell Perkins, who let Scribner's print it containing convoluted metaphors, knee-jerk similes, and numerous misspellings and grammatical and typographical errors. The book was likely never proofread at all. It was judged a failure, as was Zelda's play, *Scandalabra*.

After Scott's death in 1940, she divided her time between her mother's home in Alabama and Asheville. In August 1944, she even stayed with Thomas Wolfe's mother, who had once slammed her boardinghouse door in Scott's face. "The house is so dirty I think it best to go before atrification sets in" was Zelda's comment on the Old Kentucky Home. But it was Highland more than the city itself that brought her back. Periodically, when she sensed her condition deteriorating, she checked herself in for therapy.

One of the effects Scott's death had on Zelda was to free her to pursue her interests without recrimination. At a time when the long-term damage caused by her treatment should have left her creativity at an ebb, she began what was perhaps her most productive period. Until the end of her life, an artist kept trying to break through the fog and into the light.

Though ballet was her love, painting was her greatest talent. In the early 1940s, she produced a watercolor cycle of seventeen scenes from New York and Paris. Following this were cycles of nursery-rhyme illustrations, fairy-tale paintings, and *Alice in Wonderland* illustrations. At the end came a set of biblical tableaux created as moral lessons for her first grandchild. Her work was exhibited in both Montgomery and Asheville. It didn't place her among the first rank of artists, but she certainly didn't embarrass herself either. She also painted and decorated bowls and baskets and designed a paper-doll collection. She'd done an earlier set of dolls in which the Fitzgeralds themselves were the subjects, a ticked-off-looking Scott standing there in nothing but his underwear and a pair of fancy shoes, waiting for someone to come along and give him a set of clothes. The characters in the new set were from fairy tales.

Zelda also embarked on a second novel, "Caesar's

Things." In content, it was not far different from *Save Me the Waltz*—that is to say, it was her life story, though now with a heavy overlay of religion and psychological illness. By all accounts, her blend of surrealism and abstraction was much more successful on canvas than in a book. The deterioration of her mental powers also showed itself more clearly on the page. Zelda left forty thousand words at the time of her death.

Around eleven-thirty on the night of March 10, 1948, a fire started in the diet kitchen of Central Building at Highland. The structure had no sprinkler system or automatic alarm.

The nurse who found the blaze unlocked doors and woke patients on the lower floors, then called another building on the campus to report the situation. She did not, however, try to extinguish the flames, and she didn't notify the fire department until about a half-hour after the discovery.

Flames climbed the dumbwaiter shaft, spilled onto the landing at each floor, and ran to the roof. The stairways were blocked by fire and smoke. The exterior fire escapes, made of wood, burned quickly.

Some accounts say that the women on the uppermost floor were asphyxiated in their beds without ever having the chance to attempt an escape. Others say they tried to get out but were prevented by room doors locked from the outside and windows chained and padlocked. The only woman who managed to flee the top floor broke a window and jumped.

Twenty-two women on the lower floors escaped. Some

of them were found wandering in the woods. Altogether, nine women on the top floor perished.

According to some accounts, Zelda had until then been staying in an unlocked room and traveling freely about Asheville. What a voluntary patient was doing in a sealed ward that night is not entirely clear.

She was identified by dental records and by a single slipper trapped beneath her charred remains.

Thomas Wolfe's memory suffered a bad run of luck in July 1998, just a couple months shy of the sixtieth anniversary of his death.

On Monday, July 20, Modern Library released its list of the hundred best English-language novels of the twentieth century. F. Scott Fitzgerald received a boutonniere for his dapper lapel, *The Great Gatsby* checking in at lofty number two and *Tender Is the Night* at twenty-eight. Ernest Hemingway landed at forty-five for *The Sun Also Rises* and seventy-four for *A Farewell to Arms*. Other members of the Max Perkins stable were there—John Dos Passos for the *U.S.A.* trilogy and James Jones for *From Here to Eternity*. Henry James had three titles in the top thirty-two. Dimly remembered authors were well represented, too—Arthur Koestler, James T. Farrell, Anthony Powell, Max Beerbohm, Richard Hughes, Elizabeth Bowen, Arnold Bennett, Henry Green.

But the name of Thomas Wolfe was nowhere to be found.

"It kind of boggles the mind to think that of the 100 best titles in 20th century English literature, Thomas Wolfe isn't there," Ted Mitchell, a historian at the Thomas Wolfe Memorial, told the *Asheville Citizen-Times*. "I can't imagine a list of 20th century novels being complete without a classic like *Look Homeward, Angel*."

"It isn't exactly a John Grisham novel," explained Tom Burkhart, a volunteer at the memorial. "It's childhood emotion, impressions about an extremely dysfunctional family. Not everyone likes that."

"It doesn't really surprise me that Wolfe is not on there," said Steve Hill, the manager of the memorial. "He's never going to attain the popularity of Hemingway or Fitzgerald."

"What's in a list, anyway?" asked Mitchell. "He'd be on mine."

Less than four days later, around two o'clock in the morning on Friday, July 24, someone tossed a burning object through the dining-room window of the memorial—or at least that is the best conjecture of Asheville investigators. The act occurred on the eve of Bele Chere, the city's principal public celebration, and some suspect it was a reveler leaving a local bar after last call.

Ironically, the memorial had recently received a large appropriation for renovations, the first twenty thousand dollars of which were to buy a fire alarm, scheduled for installation just a few weeks later. Had the alarm been operational, the fire would have been confined to the dining room and done relatively little damage. As it was, it smoldered for perhaps an hour before the heat grew intense enough to break additional windows. The increased supply of oxygen set the blaze running up the walls to the upper floor and the attic, where it destroyed the support for the slate roof.

The fire was called in shortly after three. It took crews two hours to extinguish it.

Though Wolfe himself characterized the 1883 structure as "cheaply constructed," its protection as a state historic site had brought it a level of care never known during the author's day. Nearly every one of the twenty-odd rooms was described in *Look Homeward, Angel*. Indeed, the place was elevated to the status of a character.

In the minds of many, the Thomas Wolfe Memorial was the quintessential writer's home. Visitors could bring a book and read on the porch where Mabel Wolfe's guests once talked and argued, or browse the premises and examine the four thousand cataloged objects. Workers preparing for the renovation had gone to such pains as to remove up to seventeen coats of paint to determine the color scheme in Wolfe's day. Luckily, many of the most important objects, like Wolfe's typewriter, had been removed from the house preparatory to the renovation, and so were spared from the fire.

The following morning, a small crowd of spectators gathered outside the memorial to watch the firemen complete their work, to hear shock-stricken staffers try to explain what had happened, and to see a crane tear away sections of the weakened roof and lift smoke-, soot-, and water-damaged items like Ben Wolfe's bed from the upper level, then deposit them on the front lawn.

Fifteen hundred feet above Asheville, I'm having an easy time picking out downtown landmarks—the Art Deco City Building and the seventeen-story Buncombe County

Courthouse side by side not far off Pack Square; the fingerlike Jackson Building, located on the site of W. O. Wolfe's old monument shop; the Flatiron Building; McCormick Field, where Babe Ruth almost played; the Battery Park, where he convalesced, and the Grove Arcade across the street; the Basilica of St. Lawrence, said to have the largest unsupported dome in North America.

"There it is," Mike says. "Right over there. To the right of that big white building. Just behind it."

I'm ahead of him this time.

The Thomas Wolfe Memorial, newly painted its original yellow instead of its recent white, is so bright it glows. The blue tarps are gone from the outer wall of the dining room and the roof, the beautiful slate restored or—more likely—replaced. I don't see any scaffolding. It's nearly ready to go. The place looks better than it ever has.

Pat Conroy has written a wonderful twenty-page defense of Thomas Wolfe. He describes how his English teacher presented him a copy of *Look Homeward, Angel* at Christmas 1961, how he ripped straight through it three times consecutively, how he frequently caught himself holding his breath while reading. He tells about falling so deeply under Wolfe's spell that the same teacher, now worried, gave him Ernest Hemingway's *The Old Man and the Sea* as an antidote. Believing *Look Homeward, Angel* was written specially for him, he planned to present himself to Wolfe as his personal assistant, only to be devastated to learn the author had died twenty-odd years earlier. For Conroy, Wolfe is the Babe Ruth of literature, a man who swung for the fence, who wrote like his hair was on fire, who was battered by critics but never cowed, who was more courageous than other writers because he refused to hold himself back, even for his own protection.

It's enough to get you to send in your fan-club dues—until you actually read some Wolfe, that is.

In May 1937, at the end of his long-awaited visit seven and a half years after the publication of *Look Homeward, Angel*, Wolfe wrote a piece for the *Asheville Citizen-Times*. It was called, simply, "Return."

"My visit home was better than I had a right to expect," Wolfe meant to say. "I know my book hurt some feelings, but that was not my intention. At the time I wrote it, my prospects for publication were slim, and I was simply using the best material I had. I have always loved the mountains and their people, and the graciousness with which I was received these past weeks showed me how much I've missed the place."

Or something like that.

But here's how it came out: "I have been seven years from home, but now I have come back again. And what is there to say?

"Time passes, and puts halters to debate. There is too much to say; there is so much to say that never can be told;—we say it in the impassioned solitudes of youth, and of ten thousand nights and days of absence and return. But in the end, the answer to it all is time and silence: this answers all; and after this, there is no more to say."

Several columns later, he returned to wrestle with the same point: "For now I have come home again—and what is there to say? I think that there is nothing—save the silence of our speech. I think that there is nothing—save the knowledge of our glance. I think that there is nothing—save the silent and unspoken conscience in us now that needs no speech but silence, because we know what we know, we have what we have, we are what we are."

In between was an impressionistic interpretation of his boyhood, reading in part, "Here, from this little universe of time and place, from this small core and adyt of my being where once, hill-born and bound, a child, I lay at night, and heard the whistles wailing to the west, the thunder of great wheels along the river's edge, and wrought my vision from these hills of the great undiscovered earth and my America— here, now, forevermore, shaped here in this small world, and in the proud and flaming spirit of a boy, new children have come after us, as we: as we, the boy's face in the morning yet, and mountain night, and starlight, darkness, and the month of April, and the boy's straight eye."

He's like a freshman trying to fill a blue book, desperately hoping windiness and obfuscation will cover for a dearth of substance.

I've never been inside the Thomas Wolfe Memorial. One time, I arrived just after closing. Another, I was so low on money that I couldn't afford the nominal tour fee. And then I planned a visit for what turned out to be the weekend of the fire. When I woke that Saturday morning and learned the news, I decided against making the trip. By the next time I was in Asheville, the tarps were up, boards were nailed over the windows, a chain-link fence was in place, and the house was closed.

And so, too, am I absent from the grand reopening,

which falls on the same weekend my manuscript is due. I miss the rededication and ribbon cutting, the historic photograph exhibit, the celebration banquet, the guided trolley tours of Wolfe's Asheville, and the authors' presentation featuring Fred Chappell, Gail Godwin, Sharyn McCrumb, and others.

But I vow not to always be on the outside looking in. I'll give the man another chance. I'll tour the memorial. Meanwhile, I'll continue reading. I'll try to judge him by his best work instead of his worst.

I hear his short stories are good.

Acknowledgments

I've heard stories beyond number of the kindness of authors and book people, and I've witnessed many of their charitable acts firsthand. Still, I was surprised at the level of goodwill I found when writing this book.

I thank Gail Godwin, Sharyn McCrumb, Fred Chappell, Robert Morgan, Charles Price, Bill Brooks, Ann B. Ross, Joan Medlicott, Randy Russell, Jill Jones, James Seay, Bryan Aleksich, Eileen Johnson, Frankie Schelly, Steve Brown, Jack Pyle, Taylor Reese, Mart Baldwin, Susan Snowden, the unnamed members of the writer's group, Duncan Murrell, Darcy Lewis, David Toht, Bob Klausmeier, Jane Voorhees, Jerry Burns, Rob Neufeld, Mike Vidotto, Steve Hill, Peter Caulfield, Carolyn Sakowski, Elizabeth Woodman, Debbie Hampton, Tony Roberts, Martin Tucker, Ed Southern, Anne and Andrew Waters, Kim Byerly, Sue Clark, Jackie Whitman, Heath Simpson, Margaret Couch, and Pat and Ed Kirk.